FOUNDATIONS

PETER JOHN BROOKS

7 FOUNDATIONS:

ESSENTIAL CHRISTIANITY

ISBN 978-1-968804-01-5

Published by Fivestone New Media

www.bethelcornerstone.org

Wisdom has built her house, she has hewn out her seven pillars.

Proverbs 9:1

Contents

Introduction

CHRISTIANITY IS not a list of dos and don'ts. It's all about Jesus - what he did for us and how he freely gives us a relationship with God. Jesus came to deliver us from ourselves, free us from sin and evil, and connect us with Almighty God. The more we understand Jesus, the more we will experience God. And the more we experience God, the most awesome, glorious, and wonderful Person there is, the more we will find true joy and satisfaction.

"You did not choose me, I chose you" (John 15:16a).

You have this book for a reason. God wants you to be his child, and he wants you to grow spiritually. He wants you to be established in your Christian faith and to be grounded in truth.

"You shall know the truth, and the truth shall make you free" (John 8:32).

As you read this book, which is based on the Bible, you will learn important truths that will transform your life.

"The word of God is living and active, and sharper than every two-edged sword" (Hebrews 4:12).

The Bible is written by God. It is completely true. The word of God is alive. It can set you free from wrong thoughts about God and about yourself. It can free you from sinful habits that cause harm to yourself and others. It can even free you from the evil that ravages your life and the lives of the ones you love. Jesus came to save us. His salvation is perfect and complete. The more we understand God's truth, the more we will experience his glorious salvation in all aspects of our lives.

The truth of God is infinite, because God is infinite. It has many layers and levels. It is spiritually deep, high, and wide. The truth of God reflects the infinite salvation of Jesus. The salvation of Jesus is inexhaustible and limitless, and it can affect everything. We will not understand all the truth of God until we get to heaven and see God face to face, and then we will be delivered from all evil. But as we understand and accept truth now, we will experience more and more salvation.

There are 7 basic spiritual principles of Jesus Christ. The extent of our experience of Jesus depends on applying these 7 basic principles to our lives.

These 7 basic principles are listed in Hebrews 6:1-2:

> Therefore, leaving the discussion of the elementary principles of Christ, let us go on to perfection, not laying again the foundation of repentance from dead works and of faith toward God, of the doctrine of baptisms, of laying on of hands, of resurrection of the dead, and of eternal judgment. (Hebrews 6:1-2)

1. Repentance from Dead Works
2. Faith toward God
3. Water Baptism
4. Holy Spirit Baptism (Hebrews 6:2 mentions more than one baptism.)
5. Laying on of Hands
6. Resurrection of the Dead
7. Eternal Judgment

These 7 basic spiritual principles are called "the foundation" (Hebrews 6:1). They are the starting point for our faith. They reveal Jesus, who is the "chief cornerstone" in the spiritual realm (Ephesians 2:20). Everything we do spiritually must be built on Jesus Christ, who is the only way we can connect to God (John 14:6). God wants us to build our lives on Jesus Christ and grow into spiritual maturity. This begins with learning and implementing the 7 Foundations of Jesus Christ.

When we are born again, we become spiritual babies. Babies need milk in order to grow.

"As newborn babes, desire the pure milk of the word, that you may grow thereby" (1 Peter 2:2).

These 7 Foundations are "the first principles of the oracles of God." They are "milk and not solid food" (Hebrews 5:12). They contain essential spiritual nutrients that can help us grow into maturity. They prepare us to understand the deeper meat of the word of God. As we understand the 7 Foundations, we digest spiritual milk that will cause us to grow into spiritual maturity.

God wants us to go beyond elementary school and eventually get to high school, college, and even graduate school in our spiritual walk. To get a higher spiritual education and grow into spiritual maturity, we must understand the 7 Foundations. Without the 7 Foundations, it is impossible to build a strong spiritual life.

Even if we have been Christians for a long time, it is often helpful to revisit the 7 Foundations in order to make sure our spiritual basis is strong.

How to Read This Book

As you read this book, pray. God is the best teacher of spiritual truth, and he wants to teach you. It is impossible to understand the truth of God on your own. We need God to help us understand his word.

"The natural man does not receive the things of the Spirit of God, for they are foolishness to him; nor can he know them, because they are spiritually discerned" (1 Corinthians 2:14).

The word of God is understood by the spirit, not the intellect. We need God to open our spiritual eyes, so we can understand spiritual things.

When you pray and ask God to teach you, he will. The Holy Spirit dwells inside everyone who believes in Jesus, and he is our teacher.

"When He, the Spirit of truth, has come, He will guide you into all truth" (John 16:13).

There is no better teacher than the Holy Spirit, and there is no better textbook for spirituality than the Bible.

All Scripture is given by inspiration of God, and is profitable for doctrine, for reproof, for correction, for instruction in righteousness, that the man of God may be complete, thoroughly equipped for every good work. (2 Timothy 3:16)

Start a Bible Study

Using the *Seven Foundations*, you can lead a Bible study. At the end of each chapter are study notes. Start your Bible study with prayer. Then take turns reading the Bible verses. After the verses are read, discuss them using the included questions. Everyone can participate, ask questions, and share thoughts. Prayer and fellowship will happen during this time of study, and such a study might eventually become a house church.

Discern False Teachings

There are many false Christian teachings in the world. By knowing the 7 Foundations of Christ, many of these false teachings can be discerned. A building is strong only as long as its foundation is strong, and Christianity is strong only as it is built on these 7 Foundations. The Bible is the only standard by which Christianity can be measured, and if something in Christianity doesn't line up with the Bible, it's not genuine. To aid with discernment, at the end of each chapter are lists of false teachings that contradict each of these 7 Foundations.

A Hunger for God's Word

We need a hunger for the Bible so that we will want to read it. Hungry people eat. Thirsty people drink. May God bless you with a hunger for his word and a thirst for his Holy Spirit. As your spiritual appetite increases, you will find it easier to read the Bible. Try to have a regular plan of systematically reading through your Bible, and follow that plan until you finish reading the entire Bible. The NKJV might be the best Bible version for you. (For more information on the importance of the Bible and on different Bible versions, please see the *Appendix.)*

By understanding the 7 basic principles of Christianity, you will grow spiritually and encounter the reality of God. You will become the spiritually mature man or woman that God intends you to be. Your Christianity will become *alive.*

1

Repentance from Dead Works

THE FIRST FOUNDATIONAL PRINCIPLE of Christianity is repentance from dead works. Repentance is the beginning of our walk with God.

Whenever Jesus Christ came to a town, one of the first things he announced was, "Repent! For the kingdom of God has come near!" (Matthew 4:17).

The main message of John the Baptist, who prepared the way for the ministry of Jesus, was similar: "Repent!" (Matthew 3:2).

Peter, on the day of Pentecost, when asked what needed to be done, considering the facts of Christ's death and resurrection, shouted out to everyone, "Repent!" (Acts 2:38).

The Christian life starts with repentance. It's the first thing we need to do in order to follow God.

Repentance is not complicated. It just means "to turn" or "to change one's mind."

The New Testament was originally written in Greek. The Greek word for *repentance* is μετανοεο (metanoeo), which means *to change one's mind or purpose*.

Repentance doesn't mean groveling in condemnation or self-loathing. It doesn't mean beating oneself with a religious stick and getting depressed. Repentance is not penance. (Penance means paying for your sins by punishing yourself. We can never pay for our sins.) Repentance means changing your mind, changing your direction, and going in a new way.

You've been walking on a path in your life. You recognize that how you've been living is wrong because God says so. You repent and turn to a new way.

Repentance means accepting God's word. God's word is the communication of himself, and it reveals who God is and what God wants. The Bible is like a spiritual mirror (James 1:22-25) that shows us who we are in the bright light of God's holiness. When we look into the mirror of God's word, we discover aspects of our lives that God wants to change. Repentance means submitting to God and changing our lives accordingly.

We All Need to Repent

God says everyone in the world needs to repent because we all have sinned. Our oldest ancestor, Adam, was created perfect by God, but he chose to sin and was kicked out of Paradise (Genesis 3). Adam passed the inheritance of sin to all of us.

"All have sinned and lack the glory of God" (Romans 3:23).

We know that we're not perfect. We've never met anyone who is perfect. We try to excuse our mistakes by saying, "Well, no one's perfect."

"If we say that we have not sinned, we make him a liar, and his word is not in us" (1 John 1:10).

Our consciences tell us that we have sinned. Maybe we've not committed adultery, but we've looked at pornography.

which according to Jesus is the same thing. Many romance novels are no better. We've probably never killed someone, but we've hated them— and that's murder according to Jesus. We've stolen, lied, cheated, and done many other things that God didn't want us to do.

Sin Kills

The Bible compares sin to a boss. The boss, Sin, owns us, controls us, and pays us with a salary of death.

"The wages of sin is death" (Romans 6:23a).

Spiritual death means separation from God. Even if we sinned only once, we would be separated from God, but each of us has sinned much more than once. Separation from God damages people physically, emotionally, and spiritually. It ruins people eternally, and it destroys the world, producing sickness, decay, and death.

Jesus Christ is the only person who never sinned. Therefore, he didn't have to die. But Jesus died anyway. He died not for his own sins (he didn't have any) but for our sins. Then he rose up again, throwing all these sins away.

The Holy Spirit Shows Us We Must Repent

Left to ourselves, we probably wouldn't care about Jesus, and we wouldn't want to repent. We'd enjoy our sins and think that they're not that bad. The Holy Spirit has to wake us up.

"[The Holy Spirit] will convict the world of sin, and of righteousness, and of judgment" (John 16:8b).

God calls us to repent because he loves us.

"The goodness of God leads you to repentance" (Romans 2:4b).

Repentance is not about condemnation; it's about love. If you love someone, you'll want what is best for them, and God loves us more than anyone ever could.

"God so loved the world that he gave his only begotten son, that whoever believes in him should not perish but have eternal life" (John 3:16).

The great love of God compelled Jesus to come to rescue us. Jesus didn't come to tell us how bad we are. He came to give us abundant life. He is the good shepherd who leads us to green pastures and still waters. Repentance is the gateway through which we leave the ways of sin and death and enter into the green pastures of God.

"For God did not send His Son into the world to condemn the world, but that the world through him might be saved" (John 3:17).

God loves every single person in the world, and that's why he wants us all to repent.

"He is patient with you, not wanting anyone to perish, but everyone to come to repentance" (2 Peter 3:9b).

Godly Sorrow Produces Repentance

When you're traveling on a road and realize you're going in the wrong direction, you might feel sad. But rather than sit on the road crying, you turn around. It's similar with repentance. The goal of repentance is not to feel sad; the goal of repentance is to turn around.

"Godly sorrow produces repentance leading to salvation, not to be regretted; but the sorrow of the world produces death" (2 Corinthians 7:10).

The "sorrow of the world" doesn't turn us around. It just leaves us without answers, trudging onward without God. We need to get off this dead-end road; then we'll feel better. Repentance puts us on the bright path of God and opens the door to lasting joy.

"For I know the thoughts that I think toward you, says the Lord, thoughts of peace and not of evil, to give you a future and a hope" (Jeremiah 29:11).

Confession of Sin

To repent, we must confess our sins.

"If we confess our sins, he is faithful and just to forgive our sins and cleanse us from all unrighteousness" (1 John 1:9).

Confession doesn't mean weeping and wailing and condemning ourselves. Nor does it mean just saying, "I'm sorry." Instead, confession means agreement. When we confess our sins, we agree with God that what we've done is wrong, stating the specific sins we have done and agreeing with God not to do them again.

Confess your sins directly to God. Only God has the power to forgive sins and cleanse us from evil.

"He who covers his sins will not prosper, but whoever confesses and forsakes them will have mercy" (Proverbs 28:13).

In ancient Israel, priests laid hands upon the lambs' heads and confessed sins. Through confession, the sins were symbolically transferred to these lambs, and then the lambs were killed, taking the death required by God for the sins. The death of these lambs symbolized the death of Jesus.

When we confess our sins to God, we transfer our sins to Jesus, who died for our sins on the cross. After confession, God forgives our sins and cleanses us from all unrighteousness.

Sometimes we need to confess our sins to others. When we sin against someone, confession can bring healing to that person and to our relationship with that person.

Confessing to another person can help us when we are struggling against a stubborn sin. Sometimes we seem trapped by the power of sin, stuck in a cycle of sin and confess, sin and confess. When this happens, it can be helpful to confess our sin to a spiritually mature person who can pray for us and give us insight from God's word.

There are other times when we become sick because of sin. At that time, confession to another person can bring healing.

"Confess your trespasses to one another, and pray for one another, that you may be healed" (James 5:16).

Forgiveness

Repentance brings forgiveness. Forgiveness means being released. Sin incurs a spiritual debt to God, and when we confess our sins, God releases us from this debt.

God has been merciful to us by forgiving us a huge debt, and we should be merciful to others. When people sin against us, we should forgive them. Sometimes we don't feel like forgiving someone until they confess their sins, but we need to forgive them anyway. The requirement to forgive extends to everyone who has ever or will ever sin against us, whether or not they repent.

Unforgiveness

If we don't forgive, we will mar our relationship with God.

"But if you do not forgive men their trespasses, neither will your Father forgive your trespasses" (Matthew 6:15).

If we don't forgive others, God won't forgive us. Why not? Unforgiveness is a sin. As long as we hold onto the sin of unforgiveness, God cannot forgive us of that sin.

Unforgiveness is a particularly dangerous sin because it produces bitterness.

"[We must look] carefully lest anyone fall short of the grace of God; lest any root of bitterness springing up

23

cause trouble, and by this many become defiled" (Hebrews 12:15).

Bitterness produces hatred, strife, envy, and many other sins. Bitterness is an internal fountain of evil which can cause depression and even sickness. The best way to get rid of bitterness is to forgive.

As long as we don't forgive, we hold bitterness and other associated sins inside our hearts. God cannot forgive us of these sins as long as we hold onto them. But the moment we forgive others, God will forgive us of all these sins.

Repentance Heals

Once Jesus healed a lame man and then told him, "Sin no more, lest a worse thing come upon you" (John 5:14). Jesus didn't want the man to go, sin again, and get sick again. All problems in the world are because of sin. Repentance forsakes sin, which is why repentance heals.

Although sin causes problems, it is often impossible to trace specific instances of evil back to specific sins. Just because someone got sick doesn't necessarily mean his sins caused his disease. Billions of sins from billions of different people have compounded together to produce the many problems in the world today.

And as Jesus passed by, he saw a man who was blind from his birth. And his disciples asked him, saying, "Master, who did sin, this man, or his parents, that he was born blind?" Jesus answered, "Neither hath this man sinned, nor his parents: but that the works of God should be made manifest in him." (Luke 9:1-3)

The blind man didn't lack sight due to a specific sin from himself or his parents, but he was blind because he lived in a fallen and broken world. And his blindness gave Jesus an opportunity to do a miracle.

Rejecting Dead Works

When we repent, we turn away from dead works. Dead works are things we do that are contrary to God. It's obvious that sins like adultery and drunkenness are dead works, but sometimes seemingly good works are actually dead works. You might think you're a good person. Maybe you give to the poor and volunteer for charity. But it's possible for these good works to hinder you from coming to God. 'Good' people often think they are better than others, and that they don't need to repent. Many people believe they will get to heaven because of their own goodness. But all the good works in the world cannot get us to heaven.

"But we are all like an unclean thing, and all our righteousnesses are like filthy rags; we all fade as a leaf, and our iniquities, like the wind, have taken us away" (Isaiah 64:6).

Without Christ, all our works are dead, even "good" ones. They cannot give us life, nor can they pay for our sins. Everyone needs Jesus, even "good" people, for there is "none righteous, no, not one" (Romans 3:10).

"They that are whole need not a physician; but they that are sick. I came not to call the righteous, but sinners to repentance" (Luke 5:31b-32).

To go to the doctor, we must first admit we have a disease. To repent and turn to God, we must first admit we have a problem.

After trusting in Christ, the Holy Spirit changes us. All our works that were dead before, now have the potential to become alive because of the Holy Spirit. All works we do apart from God are dead, but all works God does through us are alive. Our good works will be alive if they are inspired by the Holy Spirit.

Helping Fellow Christians Repent

When fellow Christians sin against us, we have a responsibility to correct them. "If your brother or sister sins against you, rebuke them" (Luke 17:3-4). Rebuking someone means telling them that what they've done is wrong.

It's important to rebuke Christians who sin against us for three main reasons:

1. It can help them repent and be restored to God.

2. It can protect us from being harmed by that person if they are repeatedly sinning against us.

3. It can protect other people in the church from being corrupted by sin.

"A little leaven leavens the whole lump. Purge out therefore the old leaven" (1 Corinthians 5:7).

Sin spreads among people, and Jesus doesn't want sin spreading within his church. God wants sin expelled from his people so his church can be holy. "Be holy, for I am holy" (1 Peter 1:16).

We don't need to rebuke our brethren each time they sin. We must do everything in love, and "love will cover a multitude of sins" (1 Peter 4:8). In the body of Christ, there will be close relationships, and we will grate on each other. We need a lot of love. Let's be sensitive to the Holy Spirit about when to rebuke our brothers and sisters for sin, but let's not become nit-picky.

Sometimes we must separate ourselves from someone who refuses to repent. If we stay in a close relationship with such a person, we may get abused. Abuse is wrong, and it's certainly not God's will. We need to draw boundaries and protect ourselves. Although we must forgive everyone, we don't have to be in a close relationship with everyone.

Fruits of Repentance

True repentance can usually be seen. An alcoholic will throw away his bottle. An adulterer will break off his wrong relationship. Zaccheus, a greedy tax collector, gave away many of his possessions to the poor (Luke 19:8). Those who stole were called to stop stealing and start working (Ephesians 4:28-29). Witches, sorcerers, and astrologers burned their occult books (Acts 19:19).

"Bear fruits worthy of repentance," Jesus said (Matt 3:8).

Repentance means cleaning up our lives. When we repent, we'll need to go through our homes, eliminating things that might lead us astray. We might need to throw out movies, songs, video games, books, magazines, statues, pictures, or other things that are displeasing to God or that might tempt us to sin. We may need to stop going to certain places, spending money on sinful things, and wasting our time on screens.

"Make no provision for the flesh to fulfill its lusts" (Romans 13:14b).

Many movies, songs, and video games are created to entertain people through sin: murder, adultery and fornication, theft, or lawbreaking. Sin is not entertainment. Sin put Jesus on the cross and drove the nails through his hands. Let's not entertain ourselves with the things that killed Jesus.

Christians who enjoy sin are like those "who, knowing the righteous judgment of God, that those who practice such things are deserving of death, not only do the same but also approve of those who practice them" (Romans 1:32).

We should not enjoy watching people sin, whether in real life or in movies. Sin should not be fun. We are called to hate sin.

"Abhor what is evil. Cling to what is good" (Romans 12:9b).

When we repent, we'll have to start telling our friends about God, and some of our relationships might have to end. "What part has a believer with an unbeliever?" (2

Corinthians 6:15b). We'll change the way we treat our spouse, our parents, and our children.

Repentance is an ongoing process. As we grow spiritually, God will show us more and more things that he wants to change about our lives. We must stay humble and teachable, and constantly allow our lives to be molded by God's word.

Glut Yourself on God

We are not called to repent so we can reject the things of the world and become sad and depressed. We are called away from the empty things of the world so we can experience the joy that comes from God alone. Repentance is about turning away from the empty things of the world and finding true satisfaction in God.

> For My people have committed two evils: They have forsaken Me, the fountain of living waters, and hewn themselves cisterns— broken cisterns that can hold no water. (Jeremiah 2:13)

It's silly to abandon God, the fountain of living water, and try to slake our thirst by pressing our parched lips against broken vessels that have no water. Sin will always leave us empty. Repentance turns us away from the broken vessels of the world to the fountains of living water that stream out from the awesome throne of God.

> If anyone thirsts, let him come to Me and drink. He who believes in Me, as the Scripture has said, out of his heart will flow rivers of living water. (John 7:37b-38)

The Holy Spirit inside us will become living water in our souls, and we will never be thirsty again.

> Whoever drinks of the water that I shall give him will never thirst. But the water that I shall give him will become in him a fountain of water springing up into everlasting life. (John 4:14)

True joy and satisfaction is found in God alone.

> You will show me the path of life; In Your presence is fullness of joy; At Your right hand are pleasures forevermore. (Psalm 16:11)

Repentance Prepares the Way for Revival

Throughout history, repentance has been the precursor to revival and outpourings of the Holy Spirit.

In one of Peter's first messages, he said, "Repent, so that times of refreshing may come from the presence of the Lord, and He may send Jesus Christ" (Acts 3:19).

God wants to pour out his Spirit on us so we can be refreshed. He's waiting for us to repent so that we can receive the rain of the Holy Spirit. Great transformation will happen wherever the spiritual rain of the Holy Spirit falls. In addition to preparing for revival, repentance prepares the way for Jesus to return to the earth, because repentance prepares his people for his coming.

When we repent, we prepare ourselves to be filled with God's presence and power. We will encounter God, and there's nothing better than that.

~ *Prayer* ~

Heavenly Father, your way is the best way. My ways apart from you are pointless. I confess that I have often done things that were not according to your word. I have lived for myself and not for you. Help me turn away from sin. Help me clean out my life from everything that displeases you. Thank you for the blood of Jesus that cleanses me. Heal me from all the effects of my sins. Heal the people that I have hurt by sinning against them. Give me grace to forgive everyone who has sinned against me. I forgive them all and release them. Give me understanding of your word so that I can walk in your ways. In Jesus' name I pray. Amen.

Victory Over False Teachings

1. <u>No Original Sin</u>. Some churches believe that people are not born in sin; that we are all inherently good. But the Bible says that Adam's sin has corrupted us all (Romans 5:12).

2. <u>No Christian Repentance</u>. Some churches believe that it is not necessary for Christians to repent, because Jesus' blood covers all their sins - past, present, and future. Whatever sins they commit are already under the blood of Jesus, so why should they confess them? But the Bible says that we (Christians) must confess our sins (1 John 1:9), and Jesus commanded 5 out of 7 churches in the Book of Revelation to repent (Revelation 2 and 3).

3. <u>Confession to a Priest</u>. Some churches teach that the only way to get forgiveness from God is to confess sins to a priest. But the Bible says that we need to confess our sins directly to God (1 John 1:9).

4. <u>Salvation by Works</u>. Some churches believe that we are saved by works - going to church, being baptized, or doing other good things. But the Bible says that good works cannot save anyone. Only Jesus can save (Ephesians 2:8-9).

Repentance from Dead Works

Matthew 3:2, Matthew 4:17, Acts 2:38

1. What is the difference between repentance and penance? Is penance a Biblical concept?
2. Is repentance a positive or negative thing?
3. How should we call people to repent?
4. In what way is repentance both for our own sakes and for God's sake?

2 Peter 3:9, Romans 3:23, Romans 6:23, Genesis 2:16-17, Genesis 3

1. Why is everyone born into this world automatically a sinner?
2. If God wants everyone to repent, why don't they?
3. Is it possible for human free will to thwart God's will?
4. Where did evil come from?

Galatians 5:19-21, Isaiah 64:6

1. What is the fundamental difference between dead works and living works?
2. In what way can good works be dead?
3. Why do people with many good works sometimes find it hard to repent?

James 1:22-25

1. How does someone who doesn't obey the word of God deceive himself?
2. Why is it important to regularly read the Bible? How often do you read the Bible?

John 16:8

Have you ever felt convicted by the Holy Spirit? What does that feel like? How do you get rid of that feeling?

Romans 2:4

How does a call to repentance reflect the goodness of God?

2 Corinthians 7:10

1. What are some differences between godly sorrow and the sorrow of this world?
2. How does repentance take away sorrow?

1 John 1:9-10, Proverbs 28:13, James 5:16

1. What is the difference between confessing and saying "sorry"?
2. Why do we need to confess our sins directly to God?
3. Why does healing come when we confess sin?
4. Can sin lead to physical sickness?
5. Is all sickness a result of sin?
6. If a Christian dies without confessing a specific sin, will he or she go into hell? Why or why not?

Luke 17:3-4

1. What should we do when a fellow Christian sins against us?
2. Why are we commanded to rebuke believers and not unbelievers?

Matthew 18:21, Matthew 6:15, Mark 11:25, Hebrews 12:15

1. Do we need to forgive people even if they don't repent?
2. Why is forgiveness so important?
3. How does unforgiveness lead to bitterness?
4. What sins stem from bitterness?
5. Why is God unable to forgive us if we don't forgive others?
6. Have you ever held a grudge? How did that affect the other person? How did that affect you?

Matthew 18:17, 1 Corinthians 5:6-12

1. At what point should we separate from unrepentant Christians?
2. What can happen if we don't separate from them?
3. Do we ever need to separate from unbelievers?
4. How can we forgive someone and still separate from them?
5. When should we restore fellowship with someone from whom we have separated?

Matthew 3:8, Luke 19:8, Matthew 9:9, John 8:10-11, Ephesians 4:28-29, Acts 19:19

1. How do we know if repentance is genuine?
2. How do we test the fruits of repentance in our own lives?
3. Should we test the fruits of repentance in the lives of others?

Romans 13:14

1. How does a person make no provision for the flesh?
2. How can parents help their children make no provision for the flesh?

Acts 3:19

1. What are the "times of refreshing"?
2. How does repentance pave the way for revival?
3. How does repentance make it possible for Jesus to come back to the earth?

Jeremiah 2:13

1. What are some broken cisterns you have drunk from? How did that make you feel?
2. Why does the world never satisfy us?
3. How do we practically enjoy God?

Romans 2:5

1. Why is there judgment on those who don't repent?
2. Will this judgment come now, or only at the end of time?

3.   Why can't God save people who don't repent?

2

Faith Toward God

THE SECOND FOUNDATIONAL PRINCIPLE of Christ is faith toward God.

God is the most awesome and majestic being in the universe. He made us, and he's the reason we're alive. Apart from God, we have nothing that is truly valuable, but in God, we have everything we need. True joy and satisfaction can only come from God.

Knowing God starts with seeing him as he actually is. God is independent of our perceptions of him. He's an objective reality, not a subjective reality. There is not one god for you, another god for me, and a different god for a remote tribe halfway around the world. There is only one true God who made the universe.

God is not whoever someone says that he is. God is who he actually is. This means that not all religions are right. In fact, all religions are wrong except the one that accurately represents God.

Some say God is a rock. Some say he's an alien who lives on a flying saucer. Others believe God is consciousness. There are many false conceptions of God in the world.

Just as humans cannot define God, so human faith does not create God. God exists independently of whether we believe in him or not. Even if no one believed in God, he would still exist.

In order to understand God accurately, our perceptions of God must align with who he actually is. If we are to know God, he must reveal himself to us. That's why he wrote the Bible.

One and Three

The Bible reveals that there is one God. "Hear, O Israel: the Lord our God, the Lord is one!" (Deuteronomy 6:4).

This one Almighty God is revealed eternally in three persons: Father, Son, and Holy Spirit. These three persons are one God.

"For there are three that bear witness in heaven: the Father, the Word, and the Holy Spirit; and these three are one" (1 John 5:7).

Jesus pointed to this reality when he said, "Go therefore and make disciples of all nations, baptizing them in the name of the Father and of the Son and of the Holy Spirit" (Matt. 28:19). Jesus said that the Father, Son, and Holy Spirit all have one name. This common name points to the fact that these three are one God.

All three are one God. The Father is God. He is "one God and Father of all, who is over all and through all and in all" (Ephesians 4:6).

Jesus, the Son, is God. We are "looking for the blessed hope and glorious appearing of our great God and Savior Jesus Christ" (Titus 2:13).

The Holy Spirit is God. "Now the Lord is the Spirit; and where the Spirit of the Lord is, there is liberty" (2 Corinthians 3:17).

The triune nature of God is revealed throughout the Old Testament. In the Old Testament, the Hebrew word *Elohim* is used to refer to Almighty God. This is a plural word. Referring to God with a plural word points to God's unique nature - three in one.

When God made man, the Father, the Son, and the Holy Spirit communicated with each other. There was a discussion within the Godhead about the creation of mankind. In this discussion, God referred to himself with the plural pronoun *us*.

"God said, 'Let Us make man in Our image'" (Genesis 1:26).

It was similar when God decided to judge humanity at the Tower of Babel. At that time there was a similar discussion within the Godhead, and God said, "Go to, let Us go down, and there confound their language, that they may not understand one another's speech" (Genesis 11:7). Again, God used the plural pronoun *us* to describe himself.

One God in three persons may sound like a contradiction, but it's a fact revealed by the Bible. It may be hard for us to understand, but that shouldn't bother us. Our difficulty in comprehending the Trinity only proves that God is bigger than we are, and he is beyond our understanding.

Quantum physics is hard to understand. It postulates that one particle can be in two places at once. This apparent contradiction doesn't make sense to our minds, but it seems to be a proven fact. If we can believe apparently contradictory things about a tiny particle, then surely we can believe some of the amazing things that God says about himself.

God is the Creator

This awesome God, who is beyond the limitations of our own minds, is the one who created the world.

"In the beginning God created the heavens and the earth" (Genesis 1:1).

God created the universe. He made the plants and animals, the molecules and atoms. He created the world by speaking into nothing. The word of God spun all galaxies into existence. Recent research suggests there are over 2 trillion galaxies in the universe - more than grains of sand on the earth. Within each of these galaxies, there are hundreds of billions of stars. "God said, 'Let there be light, and there was light'" (Genesis 1:3). God spoke, and light came - in awesome majesty. There is power in the word of God.

God created invisible spiritual beings like angels along with invisible spiritual places like heaven. Everything, visible and invisible, was created through the power of God's word.

The world didn't just happen. Everything didn't just explode out of nothing at a Big Bang. The theory of the Big Bang not only contradicts the Bible, but it lacks scientific evidence.

All the life-forms we see today were created by God in only 4 days - after he made the stars, planets, water, and land. Life did not spontaneously arise out of some kind of primordial soup. We did not arise from rocks eroding over many years into water. This is scientifically impossible. Evolution is a lie which not only contradicts the Bible, but it also contradicts scientific facts. It takes a lot of faith to believe in the faulty theory of evolution.

Reams of complex information are contained in the DNA of each living cell. Information does not just randomly arise. It must be created by someone. All this complex information was created by God.

Evidence for God's Existence

God not only created the universe, but he also created the laws of physics and chemistry that govern the universe. These intricate laws regulate the interactions of the tiniest particles and the largest stars. Many of these laws are so complex that chemists and physicists are only now beginning to understand them. Laws don't just appear. They must be written by someone. God wrote all natural laws. He also enforces these natural laws.

The beauty and complexity of the creation, from a flower to a mountain sunset, testifies to the reality of God. The evidence for God surrounds us on all sides.

> The invisible things of him from the creation of the world are clearly seen, being understood by the things that are made, even his eternal power and Godhead; so that they are without excuse. (Romans 1:20)

The Bible says God is *clearly seen* through the creation. Atheists have no excuse for not believing in God, and agnostics have no excuse for not knowing if God exists. The creation renders every person alive inexcusable for disbelieving in God. The creation itself shouts out that God is there - that he made the world and that he upholds it until today. The existence of God ought to be an obvious fact for everyone.

Origin of Evil and Satan

The Bible says that everything in heaven and earth was created in 6 days, including the angels.

"For in six days the LORD made the heavens and the earth, the sea, and all that is in them" (Exodus 20:11a).

On day 6, God said that everything was very good (Gen. 1:31). This means that up to the 6th day, there was no evil anywhere. Angels had not yet rebelled, and Satan did not yet exist.

Sometime after day 6, one of the most powerful angels in heaven rebelled against God. This glorious being turned into the dark prince Satan. He slithered into the Garden of Eden like a snake and convinced Adam and Eve to sin. Sin suddenly separated humanity from God and unleashed evil throughout the earth, and Satan took over the world.

Blinded by Satan

Many people today don't believe in God because they are spiritually blinded by Satan.

> Whose minds the god of this age has blinded, who do not believe, lest the light of the gospel of the glory of Christ, who is the image of God, should shine on them. (2 Corinthians 4:4)

The "god of this age" is Satan, and he blinds people to the truth of God.

This spiritual blindness affects people in different ways. The co-discoverer of DNA was a man named Francis Crick. He was astounded by the complex information contained within the intricate strands of DNA. Scientifically, he knew DNA couldn't have evolved from a primordial soup, and he refused to admit that DNA came from God. So he concluded that an alien civilization must have sent DNA to earth on a spaceship (Crick, Francis: *LIFE ITSELF Its Origin and Nature,* 1981).

We don't need to believe in such fanciful myths about aliens. We need to believe the word of God. Then we can be both spiritually and scientifically accurate.

Characteristics of God

The creation tells us that God is there.

The Bible tells us what God is like. It is important for us as Christians to know the basic characteristics of the God we worship.

God is a spirit (John 4:24). Spirits are invisible and immaterial. They cannot be seen, touched, or measured. God is a Spirit, which means he can't be discovered with our five senses or measured in a laboratory. But this doesn't mean God is not real. God is very real; he's just not comprised of matter. Science can teach us about the material realm, but it can't teach us about the spiritual realm. In order to understand spiritual things, we need God to teach us. Angels are spirits. Demons are spirits. Heaven is a spiritual place. Our souls are invisible parts of this spiritual realm. We need the Bible in order to understand these spiritual realities.

The Bible says that **God is perfect.** God has no sin, darkness, or flaw. "As for God, his way is perfect" (Ps. 18:30).

"**God is light** and in Him is no darkness at all" (1 John 1:5b).

"**God is love**" (1 John 4:8b). God's very nature is love. He is kind and good.

God is omnipotent. He can do all things. "With God all things are possible" (Matthew 19:26)

God is omnipresent. He is everywhere.

> Where can I go from Your Spirit? or where can I flee from Your presence? If I ascend into heaven, You are there; if I make my bed in hell, behold, You are there.

If I take the wings of the morning, and dwell in the uttermost parts of the sea, even there Your hand shall lead me, and Your right hand shall hold me. (Psalm 139:7-10)

God is omniscient. He sees and knows everything. No secret can be hidden from him.

"For His eyes are on the ways of man, and He sees all his steps" (Job 34:21).

"The eyes of the Lord are in every place, keeping watch on the evil and the good" (Proverbs 15:3).

"Great is our Lord, and mighty in power; his understanding is infinite" (Psalm 147:5).

God is eternal. "He is before all things, and in Him all things consist" (Colossians 1:17).

"Before the mountains were brought forth, or ever You had formed the earth and the world, even from everlasting to everlasting, you are God" (Psalm 90:2).

God's Name

God has a name. God's name is **Yahweh** (see Exodus 3:14). *Yahweh* means *I am that I am*. God is the always existing one. He himself is the reason for his existence. He always has existed, and he will always exist. He is, because he is Almighty God.

There are other names for God revealed in the Bible. The name *Adonai* means *Lord. El Shaddai* means *Almighty God.* By studying these names of God, we learn more about God's nature.

The Son of God

The second person of the Trinity is the Son. The Son of God is named *Jesus,* which means *God saves* in Hebrew. The name *Jesus* is the same name as *Joshua*, the Old Testament leader who brought the Israelites into the Promised Land. Jesus is the one who brings us to heaven, our Promised Land.

Just as it is helpful to think through the characteristics of God the Father, so it is helpful to think through the characteristics of the Son.

Jesus is eternal. From eternity past, Jesus was glorified with the Father in the highest heaven. "He is before all things, and in Him all things consist" (Colossians 1:17).

Jesus is the Word of God. Someone's word is their communication; it's what they want to say. Jesus is the communication of God. Through Jesus, God speaks.

"In the beginning was the Word, and the Word was with God, and the Word was God. He was in the beginning with God" (John 1:1-2).

Jesus made the world. The Father spoke the world into existence through the Son. "All things were made through Him, and without Him nothing was made that was made" (John 1:3).

Jesus made the world, and he upholds the universe - "who being the brightness of His glory and the express image of His person, and upholding all things by the word of His power..." (Hebrews 1:3).

Jesus is God. "For in Him dwells all the fullness of the Godhead bodily" (Colossians 2:9).

Jesus is a man. "For there is one God and one Mediator between God and men, the Man Christ Jesus" (1 Timothy 2:5).

Two thousand years ago, Jesus came to the world as a man.

"[Jesus] made Himself of no reputation [emptied himself], taking the form of a bondservant, and coming in the likeness of men" (Philippians 2:7).

Jesus left his bright glory behind in heaven and came to earth as a baby. He was conceived by the power of God in the womb of a virgin named Mary.

> And the angel answered and said to [Mary], "The Holy Spirit will come upon you, and the power of the Highest will overshadow you; therefore, also, that Holy One who is to be born will be called the Son of God." (Luke 1:35)

"And the Word became flesh and dwelt among us, and we beheld His glory, the glory as of the only begotten of the Father, full of grace and truth" (John 1:14).

Jesus is the Son of God and the Son of man. He is both God and man at the same time— a perfect union of humanity and divinity. This concept, like the Trinity, is difficult for us to wrap our heads around, but the Bible reveals this truth to us. We accept it in faith, grateful that God is bigger than we are.

Jesus is the Messiah. In the Garden of Eden, God promised that someday the Seed of the woman would crush Satan's head.

"And I will put enmity between you [Satan] and the woman, and between your seed and her Seed; he shall bruise your head, and you shall bruise His heel" (Gen. 3:15).

Throughout history, ancient cultures remembered this primeval prophecy and longed for a great king who would someday destroy the terrible snake. Their memories are imperfectly preserved through art, literature, and other cultural artifacts. These memories have often formed the basis of false religions.

Jesus is that true King. He is the Messiah (*Christ* in Greek) who came to crush the head of Satan, throw him out of the world, and eliminate evil from the earth.

Jesus never sinned. Jesus "committed no sin" (1 Peter 2:22).

If someone never sins, they don't need to die. Because Jesus never sinned, he could have lived on the earth forever.

Jesus died on the cross. Even though Jesus never sinned, he died anyway. He didn't die for his own sins (because he didn't have any), he died for our sins. He died in our place.

"For He made Him who knew no sin to be sin for us, that we might become the righteousness of God in Him" (2 Corinthians 5:21).

On the cross, all sins that had ever been committed by anyone from the beginning of the world to the end of time were laid on Jesus. With all these sins on him, Jesus was separated from his Father. That's why he cried out, "My God, my God, why have you forsaken me?" (Matthew 27:46).

Only the strong Son of God could take such a heavy load.

God's wrath came on Jesus because of our sins.

"It pleased the Lord to bruise him" (Isaiah 53:10).

Jesus took our place in death. He became a sacrifice to pay our debt to God. We were redeemed "with the precious blood of Christ, as of a lamb without blemish and without spot" (1 Peter 1:19).

The blood of Christ is eternal. Jesus is the "Lamb slain from the foundation of the world" (Revelation 13:8).

The blood of Christ is eternal, which means that it stands outside of time. Since it is eternal, it can impact all points of history at once. All the animal sacrifices of the Old Testament were effective because of the eternal power of the blood of Christ. These sacrifices symbolized Christ's blood, and they drew their spiritual effectiveness from his blood.

Jesus resurrected. After dying on the cross and paying the penalty for sin, Christ rose up again. The resurrection proved that Jesus was stronger than all the sins, curses, Satanic power, demons, depression, sorrow, sickness, disease, and death that the world has ever seen or ever will see. The resurrection proves that Jesus defeated all evil. Through his resurrection, the entire creation will someday be set free from all evil corruption.

Faith Connects Us to God

Faith applies the victory of Christ to our lives. It sprinkles the spiritual blood of Jesus over us and causes us to experience salvation.

"For by grace you have been saved through faith, and that not of yourselves; it is the gift of God, not of works, lest anyone should boast" (Ephesians 2:8-9).

Faith connects us to God. When we believe that Jesus sets us free from sin, we *are* set free. When we believe that Jesus' blood cleanses us, we *are* cleansed. When we believe that Jesus died in our place, we *are* spiritually crucified with Christ. And when we believe that Jesus rose up again to give us victory over sin, we *do* rise up spiritually to live a new life. Faith makes Jesus' work on the cross effective for us personally.

Righteousness

Through faith in Jesus, we are made righteous. Being made righteous means that we are in right standing with God. We measure up to him. We are clean like he is, and we are accepted by him "that we might become the righteousness of God in Him" (1 Corinthians 5:21).

Jesus took our place in death, so we can take his place in life. He took our sins, so we can take his righteousness. He took our death, so we can take his life.

Born Again

Before trusting in Christ, we were spiritually dead, separated from God. But when we heard the gospel, the good news about how Jesus died in our place, we repented of our sins, believed in Jesus, and were born again.

We have "been born again, not of corruptible seed but incorruptible, through the word of God which lives and abides forever" (1 Peter 1:23).

The power of the word of God makes us spiritually alive to God.

"That which is born of the flesh is flesh; and that which is born of the Spirit is spirit. Marvel not that I said unto you, 'You must be born again'" (John 3:6-7).

When we were born the first time, we were born physically from our mothers. When we are born a second time, our dead spirits are made alive to God. The Holy Spirit comes inside us, and we have a spiritual heart transplant.

"I will give you a new heart and put a new spirit within you; I will take the heart of stone out of your flesh and give you a heart of flesh" (Ezekiel 36:26).

After we're born again, the Holy Spirit comes to live inside us. Every born-again Christian has the Holy Spirit inside them.

"Your body is the temple of the Holy Spirit who is in you, whom you have from God, and you are not your own" (1 Corinthians 6:19).

> Blessed be the God and Father of our Lord Jesus Christ, who according to His abundant mercy has begotten us again to a living hope through the resurrection of Jesus Christ from the dead. (1 Peter 1:3)

"Therefore, if anyone is in Christ, he is a new creation; old things have passed away; behold, all things have become new" (2 Corinthians 5:17).

Growing by Faith

When we are born again, we become spiritual babies. We are newborn babies into God's family. At this tender spiritual age, it is important for us to stay close to the Father, be in fellowship with mature believers, and keep reading the Bible.

"As newborn babes, desire the pure milk of the word, that you may grow thereby" (1 Peter 2:2).

We assimilate the word of God as we believe it and obey it.

"The righteousness of God is revealed from faith to faith; as it is written, 'The just shall live by faith'" (Romans 1:17b).

We grow spiritually through faith. All our spiritual progress in the Lord is made by faith as we increasingly believe God's word. The life of Jesus increasingly replaces our own life.

> I have been crucified with Christ; it is no longer I who live, but Christ lives in me; and the life which I now live in the flesh I live by faith in the Son of God, who loved me and gave Himself for me. (Galatians 2:20)

Part of God's Family

When we are born again, we get a new family. God becomes our Father, and other Christians become our spiritual brothers and sisters. The family of God is a huge spiritual family all over the earth, comprised of everyone who believes in Jesus.

"For you are all sons of God through faith in Christ Jesus" (Galatians 3:26).

Jesus revealed the importance of the family of God.

> While He was still talking to the multitudes, behold, His mother and brothers stood outside, seeking to speak with Him. Then one said to Him, "Look, Your mother and Your brothers are standing outside, seeking to speak with You." But He answered and said to the one who told Him, "Who is My mother and who are My brothers?" And He stretched out His hand toward His disciples and said, "Here are My mother and My brothers! For whoever does the will of My Father in heaven is My brother and sister and mother." (Matthew 12:46-50)

We need to value the family of God as Jesus values it, recognizing its importance for our own spiritual health. Only together, as a spiritual family, will we be able to fulfill our divine purpose.

Faith Accesses God

Faith is the way we access the invisible, spiritual things of God. Faith sees the invisible things of God and believes in those things. It believes in spiritual realities more than visible things. It turns heavenly reality into earthly reality.

"Now faith is the substance of things hoped for, the evidence of things not seen" (Hebrews 11:1).

Faith causes the substantiation of spiritual things. It makes them real upon the earth.

How do we get faith? "Faith comes by hearing" (Romans 10:17).

When we hear God speak, faith arises within us to believe that God will do what he said.

Faith is not just an empty hope that something might happen. A desperate quarterback might say, "I'll just heave the football down the field in faith and hope someone catches it." But this is not faith. Faith does not try to conjure up something that doesn't exist, like a Ferrari in your garage, for example. Biblical faith does not create reality. True faith is based on the already-existing spiritual reality of the word of God. It doesn't try to bend reality to human desire. It submits the human will to God. It hears from God first. Real faith originates in heaven with God and comes to us through his word.

Faith Produces Obedience

Faith obeys God's word. If we believe God, then we're going to obey him. Faith trusts God to bring his word to pass. Faith also trusts him with the results of our obedience. Faith and obedience go hand in hand.

Through faith, we become spiritually alive. And through faith, we walk with God on the new spiritual journey that he has laid out before us in his word. Each forward step in this journey is taken through faith in response to the word of God.

~ *Prayer* ~

Heavenly Father, I praise you for how awesome you are. There is none like you in heaven or on earth. Thank you for sending your Son to earth to die for my sins. Jesus paid the penalty for my sins and took them all away. Thank you for the free gift of eternal life! I am now your child! Help me to know you better, and to see you as you truly are. Deliver me from all wrong thoughts about you. Increase my faith so I can become spiritually mature. Whenever I encounter your word, help me believe it and do what it says. In Jesus' name I pray. Amen.

Victory Over False Teachings

1. <u>Jesus is Not God</u>. Some churches teach that Jesus is not God - that he is only a man. But the Bible says that Jesus Christ is God manifest in the flesh (1 Timothy 3:16).

2. <u>No Trinity</u>. Some churches believe only the Father is God, some believe only the Son is God, and some believe only the Holy Spirit is God. But the Bible says that each of these three Persons is together one God (1 John 5:7).

3. <u>Theistic Evolution</u>. Some churches believe that God guided evolution over billions of years. But the Bible says death entered into the world through Adam. Therefore, all fossils are post-Adam, and billions of years of dying creatures before Adam was impossible.

4. <u>Pre-faith Conversion</u>. Some churches believe that Christians are born again before they have faith in Jesus. But the Bible says that we must believe in Jesus in order to be born again. We are saved through faith (Ephesians 2:8), not apart from or before faith.

5. <u>New Age Faith</u>. Some churches believe that we just need to believe hard enough and strong enough, keep dreaming and thinking of the future we want, and then whatever we desire will happen. But the Bible says faith must be based on the word of God, not on human desires.

6. <u>Word Faith</u>. Some churches teach that we can define reality with our words, and whatever we speak will happen if we just have enough faith. But the Bible says God's words define the future, not our own words. True faith is based on God's word, not our own wishes.

7. <u>Salvation Without Faith</u>. Some churches believe that people can be saved without the gospel. Some believe that good people will be saved, while others believe that remote tribes who never heard about Jesus will be saved. Others believe that Jews who never believed in Jesus will be saved, or that children of believers will automatically be saved. But the Bible says that apart from faith in Jesus Christ, there is no salvation for anyone.

8. <u>Humans are gods</u>. Some churches believe that humans are gods or can become gods. But the Bible says there is only one God, and we are not him.

Deuteronomy 6:4
According to this verse, is God singular or plural?

1 John 5:7 (KJV or NKJV), Matthew 28:19, Genesis 1:26, Genesis 11:7
1. According to these verses, is God singular or plural?
2. Does the Bible ever contradict itself?
3. How should apparent discrepancies in the Bible be resolved?

The Father is God. (Ephesians 4:6)
Jesus is God. (Titus 2:13)
The Holy Spirit is God. (2 Corinthians 3:17)
1. Is it possible for us to understand everything about God?
2. Does our inability to understand something in the Bible mean it is not true?
3. Is our inability to completely understand God evidence for him or against him?
4. If someone doesn't believe in the Trinity, can he or she be a Christian?

God is Creator. (Genesis 1:1-3)
1. How did God create the world?

2. Does science contradict the Bible?
3. How does the theory of evolution contradict the Bible?
4. How does the theory of the Big Bang contradict the Bible?

Romans 1:20

1. What does the Creation reveal to everyone about God?
2. What does it mean to be without excuse?
3. Do you think remote tribes who never heard the gospel are inexcusable for rejecting God?

Psalm 53:1

Why are atheists fools?

2 Corinthians 4:4

1. What does it mean that Satan is the god of this age?
2. How has Satan blinded the minds of the unbelievers?

Genesis 1:31

1. Did God create Satan?
2. Did God create evil?
3. What kind of beings are Molech, Baal, Ashtoreth, Shiva, Krishna, and Allah?
4. Why is it important to understand God as he truly is?
5. Is it possible to worship God if we misunderstand him?

6. Is it possible to think that we're worshiping God but not actually be worshiping him?
7. What is pantheism? What is polytheism? What is monotheism? Which is right and which is wrong? How do we know?

God is a Spirit. (John 4:24)
1. Can God be seen, touched, or measured?
2. Is it possible for science to prove God? Why or why not?

God is perfect. (Psalm 18:30)
1. Many people in the world worship imperfect gods. Why?
2. How does worshiping a false god affect someone?

God is light. (1 John 1:5)
1. Have you ever experienced spiritual light or spiritual darkness? What is the difference?
2. Where does spiritual light come from?
3. Where does spiritual darkness come from?
4. How can spiritual darkness be dispelled?

God is love. (1 John 4:8)
1. Would it be correct to say that love is God?
2. What is different between the world's conception of love and the love of God?
3. Is love compatible with judgment?

God is omnipotent (all-powerful). (Matthew 19:26)

1. Can you think of anything that God cannot do?
2. Does God work miracles today?
3. Have you ever experienced a miracle?

God is omnipresent (everywhere). (Psalm 139:7-10)

Have you ever felt that God left you? (See Hebrews 13:5.)

God is omniscient (knows everything). (Job 34:21, Proverbs 15:3, Psalm 147:5)

1. Have you ever tried to keep a secret from God?
2. How does confession of sin bring things into spiritual light?

God is eternal (without beginning or end). (Colossians 1:17, Psalm 90:2)

Is Jesus eternal?

Exodus 3:14

1. What is God's name?
2. What does God's name mean?

Jesus is God. (John 1:1-3, Acts 20:28, Colossians 2:9, Philippians 2:6)

Jehovah's Witnesses and Mormons claim that Jesus is not God. Are these religions Christian?

What does the name *Jesus* mean?

Jesus is man. (Philippians 2:7, Luke 1:35, Genesis 3:15, 1 Timothy 2:5)
How does Jesus' humanity encourage us?

Jesus never sinned. (1 Peter 2:22)
Has anyone else who ever lived been perfect?

Jesus died for our sins. (2 Corinthians 5:21, Matthew 27:46, Isaiah 53:10, 1 Peter 1:19, John 3:16)
Why did the Father forsake Jesus when he was on the cross?

Revelation 13:8
In what way was Jesus slain from before the foundation of the world?

Ephesians 2:8-9
How does faith save us?

Ezekiel 36:26, 1 Peter 1:3, 1 Peter 1:23, John 3:6-7
1. Is it possible to be saved without being born again?
2. What does it mean to be born again?
3. How can a person be born again?

1 Peter 2:2
1. How do spiritual babies grow?
2. What is spiritual milk? How can someone drink this milk?

2 Corinthians 5:17, Galatians 2:20, Romans 6:20-22

Will Christians sin? Why or why not?

1 Corinthians 6:17, 1 Corinthians 6:19
1. What is the function of a temple?
2. What should a temple of the Holy Spirit be like?

Romans 1:17, Rom. 10:17, Hebrews 11:1, James 1:22
1. What is the difference between the world's concep-tion of faith and the Bible's conception of faith?
2. How does faith help us grow in Christ after we are born again?

Have you been born again? If so, when?

3

Water Baptism

AFTER REPENTING AND BELIEVING in Jesus, we need to be baptized in water. Water baptism is the third foundational principle of Jesus Christ.

John the Baptist was sent by God to baptize people in water. Crowds came to hear his message of repentance at the Jordan River and be baptized. Even Jesus was baptized there by John.

"When all the people were baptized, it came to pass that Jesus also was baptized..." (Luke 3:21a).

Jesus gave us an example of being baptized, showing us that we should also be baptized. Jesus baptized people in water (John 3:22). His disciples baptized people. He commanded all his followers to be baptized in water.

> Go therefore and make disciples of all the nations, baptizing them in the name of the Father and of the Son and of the Holy Spirit, teaching them to observe all things that I have commanded you; and lo, I am with you always, even to the end of the age. Amen. (Matthew 28:20)

It is important for every Christian to be baptized. Baptism is not a religious ritual. It's a powerful spiritual experience. Whenever we obey God, we grow spiritually, and when we submit to the Lord by being baptized, we will grow. All our problems won't be solved by being baptized, but when we are baptized we will be blessed, and our spiritual foundation will be strengthened.

Baptism Represents Salvation

Jesus said, "He who believes and is baptized will be saved; but he who does not believe will be condemned" (Mark 16:16). It might appear from this verse that baptism is the same as salvation, and we need to be baptized in order to be saved. But we don't need to be baptized to be saved. We believe in Jesus to be saved. The thief on the cross was saved, even though he wasn't baptized. He believed in Jesus, and then he was reconciled to God. Jesus told him, "Today you will be with me in Paradise" (Luke 23:43).

This verse shows that baptism is a reflection of our salvation. It is a symbol that represents that we are born again.

Baptism is important because it is a divine-instituted symbol which represents three different things that happen to us when we are born again:

1. Being cleansed from sin
2. The burial of the old, sinful man
3. Being placed into Christ

Baptism Symbolizes Being Cleansed from Sin

First, baptism symbolizes being cleansed from our sins.

> There is also an antitype [to the flood of Noah] which now saves us - baptism (not the removal of the filth of the flesh, but the answer of a good conscience toward God), through the resurrection of Jesus Christ. (1 Peter 3:20-21)

When the flood of Noah came, the old world was washed clean with a flood of water. This is a picture of how our sins are washed away when we trust in Christ. Baptism symbolizes taking a spiritual bath and washing away spiritual filth from our lives. Because of this powerful symbolism, Peter says that baptism "now saves us." Of course, faith saves us, not baptism, but being cleansed from sin is represented by water baptism, and that's Peter's point.

"And now why are you waiting? Arise and be baptized, and wash away your sins, calling on the name of the Lord" (Acts 22:16).

Baptism Symbolizes Burial

The second thing that water baptism symbolizes is burial of the old man. In the Bible, our sinful self is referred to as the "old man." The old man is who we are apart from Christ. The old man cannot be reformed. No matter how much we try to change our old self and make it better, we cannot. Death is the only answer for the old man, and when we first trust in Christ, our old man is symbolically crucified along with Jesus on the cross.

> I have been crucified with Christ; it is no longer I who live, but Christ lives in me; and the life which I now live in the flesh I live by faith in the Son of God, who loved me and gave Himself for me. (Galatians 2:20)

When someone dies, his body is buried. When we trust in Christ, our old sinful man is killed. Water baptism is the symbolic burial of the old man. This is why the Bible says

Christians have been "buried with Him in baptism" (Colossians 2:12).

> Or do you not know that as many of us as were baptized into Christ Jesus were baptized into His death? Therefore we were buried with Him through baptism into death, that just as Christ was raised from the dead by the glory of the Father, even so we also should walk in newness of life. For if we have been united together in the likeness of His death, certainly we also shall be in the likeness of His resurrection, knowing this, that our old man was crucified with Him, that the body of sin might be done away with, that we should no longer be slaves of sin. For he who has died has been freed from sin. (Romans 6:3-7)

Through baptism, our old, fleshly, sinful person is symbolically buried. We go under the water, renouncing sin and burying our old life, and we come out of the water to live a new life in God.

Water Baptism Symbolizes Being Put into Christ

The third thing water baptism symbolizes is being placed into the body of Christ. When we are born again, we become part of Jesus' body. "For we are members of His body, of His flesh and of His bones" (Ephesians 5:30). The

Holy Spirit puts us into Christ at the moment of salvation.

"For as many of you as were baptized into Christ have put on Christ" (Galatians 3:27).

Being baptized in water symbolizes being placed into the body of Christ.

"For by one Spirit we were all baptized into one body - whether Jews or Greeks, whether slaves or free - and have all been made to drink into one Spirit" (1 Corinthians 12:13).

We become part of Christ's body at the moment of salvation, and this is symbolized by being baptized. The most powerful place in the universe is *in Christ*. Jesus Christ is far above every other power, and he has authority over everything. When we are in Christ, we are spiritually in the place that he is. His authority becomes our authority.

> Even when we were dead in trespasses, [He] made us alive together with Christ (by grace you have been saved), and raised us up together, and made us sit together in the heavenly places in Christ Jesus. (Ephesians 2:5-6)

Timing of Baptism

When someone is born again, he or she is immediately qualified to be baptized.

An Ethiopian official, riding in his chariot, heard and understood the gospel through Philip. Immediately, he stopped his chariot and got baptized on the roadside.

> "See, here is water. What hinders me from being baptized?" Then Philip said, "If you believe with all your heart, you may." And he answered and said, "I believe that Jesus Christ is the Son of God." So he commanded the chariot to stand still. And both Philip and the eunuch went down into the water, and he baptized him. (Acts 8:36-38)

When someone believes in Jesus, he is born again. Then he should immediately be baptized.

When Peter preached on the day of Pentecost, 3,000 people believed. They were immediately baptized. "Then those who gladly received his word were baptized; and that day about three thousand souls were added to them" (Acts 2:41).

When Peter preached the gospel to Cornelius' family and friends, many of them believed in Jesus. Immediately, they were baptized.

> Then Peter answered, "Can anyone forbid water, that these should not be baptized who have received the Holy Spirit just as we have?" And he commanded them to be baptized in the name of the Lord. (Acts 10:47-48)

When Paul and Silas preached to the Philippian jailer and his household, they believed the gospel. Immediately, they were baptized.

> So they said, "Believe on the Lord Jesus Christ, and you will be saved, you and your household." Then they spoke the word of the Lord to him and to all who were in his house.... And immediately he and all his family were baptized. (Acts 16:31-33)

Throughout the New Testament, people didn't need to wait to be baptized. They didn't need to go to special classes or study a bunch of books. They just needed to be born again.

Mode of Baptism

Baptism in the New Testament was done by fully immersing a person in water. A believer went completely under the water, symbolizing that all his sins were cleansed, the old man was totally buried, and he now belonged completely to Christ. Then he came up out of the water, symbolizing that he was cleansed from sin, his flesh was dead, and he was going to live a new life in Christ. Baptism should be done in the same way today, by full immersion.

In the New Testament, water baptism was done in the name of Jesus (see Acts 2:38; 8:12; 8:16; 10:48; 19:5). Jesus said that every Christian should be baptized in the name of the Father, Son, and Holy Spirit (Matthew 28:19). Apparently, being baptized in the (singular) name of the Father, Son, and Holy Spirit is the same as being baptized in the name of Jesus. This is because Jesus is God, and Jesus is one name for God.

The name of Jesus is higher than any other name.

> Therefore God also has highly exalted Him and given Him the name which is above every name, that at the name of Jesus every knee should bow, of those in heaven, and of those on earth, and of those under the earth, and that every tongue should confess that Jesus

Christ is Lord, to the glory of God the Father. (Philippians 2:9-11)

All God's children have spiritually taken the name of the "Lord Jesus Christ, from whom the whole family in heaven and earth is named" (Ephesians 3:15).

Jesus is the only name that can save us.

"There is no other name under heaven given among men by which we must be saved" (Acts 4:12b).

Baptizing "in the name of Jesus," or "in the name of the Father, Son, and Holy Spirit," or even "in the name of the Father, Son, and Holy Spirit which is Jesus" is all basically the same thing.

False Baptisms

Baptism is only effective when it is done after someone is born again. This is because baptism is an outward symbol of an inward spiritual change, and if this inward change has not happened, then the outward symbol becomes meaningless. Just like wearing a wedding ring is meaningless if a person is unmarried, so there is no point in baptizing people who are not born again.

What about infants? Babies cannot be born again because they cannot understand the gospel. Therefore, babies should not be baptized. As soon as children are old enough to understand the gospel and be born again, they are old enough to be baptized.

Baby baptism can be spiritually dangerous because it might mislead people by giving them a false assurance of salvation. A person might think, "I've been baptized as a baby, and therefore I'm already saved." They then think they don't need to be born again.

If you were baptized as an infant or even as an adult when you were not born again, your baptism is not Biblical. If since that time you have believed in Jesus and been born again, you should now be baptized.

One Baptism

There is one common baptism for all believers, all around the world.

"There is one body and one Spirit, just as you were called in one hope of your calling; one Lord, one faith, one baptism; one God and Father of all, who is above all, and through all, and in you all" (Ephesians 4:4-6).

If a person was baptized after he was born again, and that baptism was done by someone who is born again, then that is a true baptism that is recognized by God. A baptism in America is just as effective as a baptism in Timbuktu - and vice versa. As long as we were baptized after we were born again by a born-again believer, then our baptism is effective. Every Christian should be baptized in water, so their spiritual foundation can be more complete.

~ *Prayer* ~

Dear God, thank you for the powerful transformation that happened in my life when I trusted in your Son for salvation. My sins were washed away, the old man of my flesh was killed, and you made me part of the body of Christ. I am a new creation. Old things have passed away, and all has become new. This is all wonderfully symbolized by water baptism. Praise you for who I am in Christ, and for the riches I have in Jesus. Help me to live in my new identity as a child of God, by the power of Jesus. In his name I pray. Amen.

Victory Over False Teachings

1. Infant Baptism. Some churches believe that babies should be baptized. But the Bible says that only those who trust in Christ can be baptized (Acts 8:37).

2. <u>Baptismal Regeneration</u>. Some churches believe that when someone is baptized, they are saved. But the Bible says we are saved by faith, not by baptism.

3. <u>Sprinkling</u>. Some churches believe that baptism should be done by sprinkling. But the Greek word *baptizo* means to immerse.

4. <u>Baptism Must be Done by Clergy</u>. Some churches believe that baptism must only be done by a professional priest or member of the "clergy." But the Bible says every believer is a priest.

5. <u>Re-baptism to Join a Denomination</u>. Some churches teach that only baptisms done in their denomination are valid; therefore, anyone who comes to their group must be re-baptized. But the Bible says all Christian baptisms are valid, as long as both the baptizer and the one being baptized are born again.

6. <u>Water Baptism is No Longer Needed</u>. Some churches believe that water baptism is not necessary for Christians today. They believe that water baptism is only a spiritual truth that is not to be done literally. But the apostles actually baptized people in water throughout the New Testament, and Jesus commanded every believer to be literally baptized (Matthew 28:19).

Water Baptism

Mark 1:4-5
1. How did the water baptism of John the Baptist prepare people for Jesus' ministry?
2. How is repentance connected to water baptism?

Luke 3:21
Why did Jesus get baptized?

Mark 16:16, Luke 23:42-43
1. Is it necessary to be baptized in order to be saved?
2. Why should we be baptized?
3. What are some results of being baptized?

Acts 8:36-38, Acts 10:47-48, Acts 16:31-33, Acts 2:41
1. Who is qualified for baptism?
2. When should a person get baptized?
3. Do we need to take classes before being baptized?
4. Is infant baptism Biblical?
5. How could belief in infant baptism hinder someone from being born again?
6. Is it ever appropriate to be re-baptized?
7. Do we need to be baptized in a religious building by "clergy"?
8. Should baptism be done by sprinkling or by immersion?

1 Pet. 3:20-21, Acts 22:16

1. How does water baptism symbolize being cleansed from sin?
2. When are our sins washed away?

Colossians 2:12, Romans 6:3-7

1. When is our old man killed?
2. How does being baptized symbolize being buried?
3. What happens if a dead body is not buried?

Galatians 3:27, 1 Corinthians 12:13, Ephesians 5:30

1. When do we become part of the body of Christ?
2. How does being baptized represent becoming part of the body of Christ?

Matthew 28:19-20

What is the name of the Father, Son, and Holy Spirit?

Philippians 2:9-11, Ephesians 3:15, Acts 4:12

1. What does it mean that the name of Jesus is the most powerful name?
2. What does this powerful name mean for us practically?

Acts 2:38, 8:12, 8:16, 10:48, 19:5

1. Is it wrong to be baptized in the name of Jesus? Why or why not?

2. Have you ever been baptized? If so, when? Was this baptism Biblical?

4

Holy Spirit Baptism

THE FOURTH FOUNDATIONAL PRINCIPLE of Christ is baptism in the Holy Spirit. Both baptisms, water and Spirit, are essential for spiritual growth. Both are included in "the teaching of baptisms" (Hebrews 6:2). (The word *baptisms* in Hebrews 6:2 is the word *baptismos* in Greek, and *baptisms* is the correct translation of this word into English.)

John the Baptist taught two baptisms. He said that he baptized in water, but Jesus would baptize in the Holy Spirit.

> I indeed baptize you in water unto repentance: but He that comes after me is stronger than I, whose sandals I am not worthy to bear: He shall baptize you in the Holy Spirit and fire. (Matthew 3:11)

People baptize other people in water, plunging them in water to symbolize death to sin. Jesus baptizes people in the Holy Spirit, immersing them in the Holy Spirit so they can live the Christian life in the power of God.

Every Born-Again Believer has the Holy Spirit Inside

When someone is born again, the Holy Spirit comes inside him. His dead spirit is made alive and joined to the Holy Spirit. "But he who is joined to the Lord is one spirit with Him" (1 Corinthians 6:17).

At the moment of salvation, we are "sealed" with the Holy Spirit (2 Cor. 1:21-22, Eph. 1:13-14, Eph. 4:30). Our bodies become "temples" of the Holy Spirit (1 Cor. 6:19). The indwelling Spirit is the "downpayment" of our inheritance from God (2 Cor. 5:5), and it is proof that we belong to Christ (Rom. 8:9).

Every born-again believer has the Holy Spirit inside. But not every born-again believer is baptized in the Holy Spirit. Every believer has the Holy Spirit in measure, but not every believer is filled to the brim with the Holy Spirit.

The baptism in the Holy Spirit is different from being indwelt by the Holy Spirit when we are born again. Being baptized in the Holy Spirit means being filled to overflowing with the Holy Spirit for the first time.

Jesus was Filled with the Holy Spirit

The life of Jesus gives us a pattern. Jesus was perfectly holy from his mother's womb. Obviously, Jesus was saved, for he was never lost. He had the Holy Spirit inside him. Yet, for thirty years, he was not doing public ministry.

When he was about thirty years old, Jesus was baptized in water. After this, the Holy Spirit descended on him, and he was filled with the Holy Spirit (Luke 4:1). Then, Jesus began working miracles and publicly teaching God's word.

If Jesus needed to be filled with the Holy Spirit before beginning his ministry, how much more do we need to be filled with the Holy Spirit?

The Early Disciples were Baptized in the Holy Spirit

Before the Day of Pentecost, the 120 disciples believed in Jesus. They were born again and baptized in water. And like all born-again believers, they had the Holy Spirit inside. Jesus "breathed on them, and said to them, 'Receive the Holy Spirit'" (John 20:22).

Even though the disciples were saved and had the Holy Spirit inside, they still needed to be baptized in the Holy Spirit.

Jesus told them:

> Wait for the promise of the Father...for John truly baptized with water, but you shall be baptized with the Holy Spirit not many days from now...you shall receive power after that the Holy Spirit is come upon you and you shall be witnesses. (Acts 1:4-8)

Jesus defines the baptism of the Holy Spirit as receiving spiritual power to do effective ministry. If the disciples had rushed out of the Upper Room and tried to do ministry in their own strength, it wouldn't have worked. Jesus told them to "stay in the city until you have been clothed with power from on high" (Luke 24:49).

Ten days later, on the Day of Pentecost at about 9:00 in the morning, the power came. The 120 disciples were baptized in the Holy Spirit.

> And when the day of Pentecost was fully come, they were all with one accord in one place. And suddenly there came a sound from heaven as of a rushing mighty wind, and it filled all the house where they were sitting. And there appeared unto them cloven

tongues like as of fire, and it sat upon each of them. And they were all filled with the Holy Spirit, and began to speak with other tongues, as the Spirit gave them utterance. (Acts 2:1-4)

The 120 were "all filled with the Holy Spirit" (Acts 2:4). They already had the Holy Spirit inside them, but now they were filled to overflowing with the Spirit. Baptism in the Holy Spirit marks the first time a believer is filled with the Holy Spirit.

The baptism in the Holy Spirit gave them power that transformed them. They were no longer timid and afraid. They burst out of the Upper Room and preached the gospel boldly in Jerusalem, and three thousand people were saved.

The Results of Being Baptized in the Spirit

When we are born again, we begin to experience the wonderful blessings of the Holy Spirit. We understand the Bible, appreciate Christian fellowship, experience God's presence and leading, and bear spiritual fruit. After being baptized in the Holy Spirit, the work of the Holy Spirit within us multiplies. We bear more spiritual fruit, understand the Bible better, receive clearer leading from God, and can participate more effectively in church. We are empowered to be God's witnesses. Baptism in the Holy Spirit expands the work of the Holy Spirit in our lives.

A Promise for All Believers

When Peter preached on the Day of Pentecost, he said that God was fulfilling an ancient prophecy from Joel.

> And afterward, I will pour out my Spirit on all people. Your sons and daughters will prophesy, your old men will dream dreams, your young men will see visions. Even on my servants, both men and women, I will pour out my Spirit in those days. I will show wonders in the heavens and on the earth, blood and fire and billows of smoke. (Joel 2:28-30)

Peter said the baptism of the Holy Spirit is for every believer.

> Then Peter said to them, "Repent, and let every one of you be baptized in the name of Jesus Christ for the remission of sins; and you shall receive the gift of the Holy Spirit. For the promise is to you and to your children, and to all who are afar off, as many as the Lord our God will call." (Acts 2:38-39)

The commands *repent* and *be baptized* are in the aorist tense in Greek, which means that this action is to be completed and made part of our past experience. After doing this – repenting and being baptized in water – *you shall receive the gift of the Holy Spirit.* The promise about the Holy Spirit is in the future tense – it's something that will happen after the first two things are done.

Peter was basically saying that if you repent and are baptized in water, you too will receive the gift of the Holy Spirit. "Receiving the gift of the Holy Spirit" does not refer to the portion of the Holy Spirit that we receive when we are born again, for that is necessarily received prior to water baptism. Instead, it refers to the baptism of the Holy Spirit, which happens *after* being born again. The baptism of the Holy Spirit is subsequent to salvation, as we see with the experience of the 120 and of other disciples in the book of Acts.

Samaritans were Baptized in the Holy Spirit

Philip the evangelist went to Samaria and preached the gospel.

"When they believed Philip as he preached the things concerning the kingdom of God and the name of Jesus Christ, both men and women were baptized" (Acts 8:12b).

The Samaritans believed the gospel and were born again. Then they were baptized in water.

> Now when the apostles were at Jerusalem heard that Samaria had received the word of God, they sent unto them Peter and John: who, when they were come down, prayed for them, that they might receive the Holy Spirit (for as yet He was fallen upon none of them, only they were baptized in the name of the Lord Jesus). Then laid they their hands on them, and they received the Holy Spirit. (Acts 8:14-17)

Later, the apostles came and laid hands on these born-again believers. The Holy Spirit fell on them, and they were baptized in the Holy Spirit.

Paul was Baptized in the Holy Spirit

Saul saw the risen Christ on the Damascus road. Shocked by the power of Jesus, Saul called Jesus "Lord." A little while later, God told Ananias to pray for Saul so he could be filled with the Holy Spirit.

> And Ananias went his way and entered the house; and laying his hands on him he said, "Brother Saul, the Lord Jesus, who appeared to you on the road as you came, has sent me that you may receive your sight and be filled with the Holy Spirit." Immediately there fell from his eyes something like scales, and he received his sight at once; and he arose and was baptized. (Acts 9:17-18)

Saul had already been born again before he met Ananias. That's why Ananias called Saul his "brother." Ananias would not have called Saul his spiritual brother if he had not been born again. Ananias was not sent to Saul to share the gospel with him, but to lay hands on him so he could be healed and be baptized in the Holy Spirit.

When Ananias laid hands on Saul, he was baptized in the Holy Spirit (which means he was filled with the Holy Spirit for the first time). Scales fell from his eyes, and he saw clearly. Similarly, when we are baptized with the Holy Spirit, spiritual scales will fall from our eyes. We will see and understand spiritual things like never before, and the spiritual realm will become more real.

Cornelius' Household was Baptized in the Holy Spirit

Cornelius called for Peter to come and share the gospel with his household. He came and preached to Cornelius' family and friends.

> While Peter yet spake these words, the Holy Spirit fell on all them who heard the word. And they of the circumcision who believed were astonished, as many as came with Peter, because on the Gentiles also was poured out the gift of the Holy Spirit. For they heard them speak with tongues, and magnify God. Then answered Peter, "Can any man forbid water, that these

should not be baptized, who have received the Holy Spirit as well as we?" And he commanded them to be baptized in the name of the Lord. (Acts 10:44-48)

While Peter was speaking to Cornelius' household, they believed the gospel and were born again. Almost immediately, they were baptized in the Holy Spirit.

Disciples at Ephesus are Baptized in the Holy Spirit

We see another example of believers being baptized in the Holy Spirit in Acts 19. Again, this occurred after they were born again.

And it came to pass, that…Paul…came to Ephesus, and finding certain disciples, he said unto them, "Have you received the Holy Spirit since you believed? (Acts 19:1-2)

Paul asked if these disciples had "received the Holy Spirit since they believed." Paul wasn't asking if they were born again and had the Holy Spirit inside them, because he assumed that they already believed and were born again. He knew the Holy Spirit indwells every true believer. Instead, Paul was asking them if they had been baptized in the Holy Spirit *since* they had believed.

They gave Paul a surprising answer. "We have not so much as heard whether there be any Holy Spirit" (Acts 19:3).

After asking another question, Paul discerned that these "disciples" weren't even born again! They were followers of John the Baptist.

Paul quickly shared the gospel with them. They believed, were born again, and were baptized in water.

"And when Paul had laid hands upon them, the Holy Spirit came on them; and they spake with tongues and prophesied" (Acts 19:6).

After being born again and baptized in water, they were baptized in the Holy Spirit.

Not all Born-Again Believers are Baptized in the Holy Spirit

Both baptisms - water and Spirit - are subsequent to salvation. People can be born again for many years and never experience either baptism. Some Christians have never been baptized in water. Maybe their church never taught them about being baptized in water, or maybe they were baptized as babies and never saw the need to be baptized in water after being born again.

In a similar way, many Christians have never been baptized in the Holy Spirit. Maybe they have never heard about the baptism of the Holy Spirit. No one taught them about it, and they've never studied what the Bible says about it.

It's important for each believer to have both baptisms, water and Spirit, if they are to fulfill their potential in God. Satan attacks the teaching of both baptisms and tries to hinder Christians from experiencing both of them. We must be willing to break through this opposition and experience both baptisms, for only in this way will we be able to fulfill our potential in God.

Three Ways People are Baptized in the Holy Spirit

The Scriptures reveal that people are baptized in the Holy Spirit in primarily three ways.

1. They may be baptized in the Holy Spirit when a more mature Christian lays hands upon them, as happened with the Samaritans, with Saul, and with the disciples in Ephesus. This is the most common way that people are baptized in the Holy Spirit.

2. They may be baptized in the Holy Spirit while they are praying, as with the first disciples in the Upper Room.

3. They may be baptized in the Holy Spirit while they hear the Word of God being preached, as with Cornelius' household.

The order of the baptisms may be flipped. Sometimes water baptism is first (as with the Samaritans, the first disciples, and at Ephesus). Sometimes Spirit baptism is first (as with Saul and at Cornelius' household).

But regardless of whether water baptism is first or Spirit baptism is first, both baptisms are subsequent to being born again.

Asking for the Baptism of the Holy Spirit

God is not going to force anyone to be baptized in the Holy Spirit. The Holy Spirit is gentle like a dove. He doesn't force himself on anyone. It's the same with water baptism. No one can be forced to be baptized in water. He must desire water baptism of his own accord and ask someone to baptize him. Similarly, we must ask Jesus to baptize us in the Holy Spirit.

> If a son asks for bread from any father among you, will he give him a stone? Or if he asks for a fish, will he give him a serpent instead of a fish? Or if he asks for an egg, will he offer him a scorpion? If you then, being evil, know how to give good gifts to your children,

how much more will your heavenly Father give the
Holy Spirit to those who ask Him. (Luke 11:11-13)

Jesus said that God's children need to ask him to give
them more of the Holy Spirit. They shouldn't think that
they have all there is of the Holy Spirit, and they don't
need any more. When we ask, we will receive, because
God loves to give more of the Holy Spirit to his children.

Needless Fear of Demons

People are sometimes afraid to ask God for the baptism
of the Holy Spirit because they are afraid that they will
get a demon instead of the Holy Spirit. This is an unnec-
essary fear.

Jesus says that parents won't trick their children by giving
them a scorpion instead of an egg, or a snake instead of a
fish. In the Bible, scorpions and snakes symbolize evil
spirits (Luke 10:19). God won't trick his children when
they ask for the baptism of the Holy Spirit by allowing
them to receive a demon instead. This would be completely contrary to the nature of God.

We can ask God in confidence for the baptism of the
Holy Spirit, believing that he will fulfill his promise. The
devil is a liar. He especially lies about the baptism of the
Holy Spirit because it is key to Christian power and spiri-

tual success. Reject the devil's lies and embrace the word of God. Each Christian should ask God to baptize him or her with the Holy Spirit, and then receive the baptism of the Holy Spirit in faith.

Spiritual Gifts

When we are baptized in the Holy Spirit, we will begin to operate spiritual gifts. Spiritual gifts are supernatural abilities from God. Every Christian who has been baptized in the Holy Spirit has at least one spiritual gift.

"As each one has received a gift, minister it to one another, as good stewards of the manifold grace of God" (1 Peter 4:10).

Spiritual gifts are given in order to build up the church, which is compared to a body. Each part of the body has a different function, and each part must function for the whole to be healthy. As the spiritual gifts within the body of Christ operate, the body of Christ will grow.

> The whole body, joined and knit together by what every joint supplies, according to the effective working by which every part does its share, causes growth of the body for the edifying of itself in love. (Ephesians 4:16)

There are several different spiritual gifts listed in 1 Corinthians 12:8-10.

Tongues is speaking in a language that the speaker doesn't know.

Interpreting tongues is interpreting an unknown language, and often operates to interpret the spiritual gift of tongues.

Prophecy means speaking what God is saying now. Prophecy can be about the past, present, or future.

Word of wisdom is supernatural counsel from God.

Word of knowledge reveals hidden or secret things.

Helps is assisting people by the power and wisdom of God.

Healing is supernatural power to heal sickness.

Miraculous power causes obvious supernatural events to take place.

Discernment is the ability to discern which spirit is from God and which spirit is not from God.

The spiritual gifts allow us to build up the church through God's power so it can grow and fulfill its mission.

When someone is baptized with the Holy Spirit, God's Spirit fills him for the first time, and he may manifest a gift of the Spirit, whether speaking in tongues, prophecy, or another gift.

Each spiritual gift is good, and we are commanded to desire these spiritual gifts. "Earnestly desire spiritual gifts" (1 Corinthians 14:1).

Speaking in Tongues

Speaking in tongues has become controversial, and different churches believe different things about it. Some churches believe that speaking in tongues is so bad that if a person speaks in tongues, he is deceived or possibly even demonized. Other churches believe that speaking in tongues is so important that unless someone speaks in tongues, that person cannot be baptized in the Holy Spirit. All these teachings must be measured by the Bible.

First of all, the Bible says speaking in tongues is good. Paul wanted everyone to speak in tongues. He said, "I would that you all spoke in tongues" (1 Corinthians 14:5).

Paul spoke in tongues himself, and he was glad he did. He said, "I thank my God I speak with tongues more than you all" (1 Corinthians 14:18).

Speaking in tongues is good because it helps people grow spiritually. "He who speaks in a tongue **edifies himself**" (1 Corinthians 14:4).

No one should be stopped from speaking in tongues. "Therefore, brethren, desire earnestly to prophesy, and **do not forbid to speak with tongues**" (1 Corinthians 14:39).

People will often speak in tongues when they are baptized in the Holy Spirit (as in Acts 2:4, 10:46, 19:6). But people don't have to speak in tongues when they are baptized in the Holy Spirit. Paul asks, "Do all speak in tongues?" (1 Corinthians 12:30). This is a rhetorical question, and the answer is "No." Not everyone is going to speak in tongues, even if they are baptized in the Holy Spirit.

No one should feel obligated to speak in tongues. Compelling people to speak in tongues can create confusion. The gift of tongues is not received by repeating the tongues that another person is speaking. Nor is this gift received by manufacturing gibberish with the mind. Speaking in tongues happens by inspiration of the Holy Spirit.

Tongues do not have to be actual human languages. Some tongues are unknown to anyone.

"For he who speaks in a tongue does not speak to men but to God, for **no one understands him**; however, in the spirit he speaks mysteries" (1 Corinthians 14:2).

Sometimes a tongue might be the language of angels (1 Corinthians 13:1).

Tongues that are not understood by other people cannot help them, for it's just the sound of gibberish. To help others, tongues must be interpreted (see 1 Corinthians 14:27-28). Interpretation of tongues is a spiritual gift that enables someone to understand the meaning of tongues through the Holy Spirit and speak it to others so they can understand what is being said (see 1 Corinthians 14:27-28).

Being Filled with the Spirit
Being baptized in the Holy Spirit means being filled with the Holy Spirit for the first time. After this, we need to be filled repeatedly with the Holy Spirit.

"Be filled with the Spirit" (Ephesians 5:18b).

The book of Acts gives several examples of believers who were already baptized with the Holy Spirit being subsequently filled with the Holy Spirit again (Acts 4:8, 4:31, 7:55, 13:9, 13:52). These fillings of the Holy Spirit gave these disciples special power for ministry to meet specific needs.

The baptism of the Holy Spirit, like water baptism, is essential to grow in the Lord and fulfill our divine purpose. Without Holy Spirit baptism, we will be spiritually limited. All Christians should be baptized in the Holy Spirit so they can be empowered to fulfill God's plan for their lives, and so they can continue to strengthen their spiritual foundation.

~ *Prayer* ~

Heavenly Father, Thank you for the gift of your Holy Spirit. I want more of your Holy Spirit in my life. Fill me with your Spirit. Increase my hunger for you. Help me to live in the Spirit and not in the flesh. I want to live a supernatural life. Please give me your spiritual gifts, especially the gift of prophecy. Help me grow strong in your Spirit, that I may win victories for your kingdom upon this earth. In Jesus' name I pray. Amen.

Victory Over False Teachings

1. The Baptism of the Holy Spirit Equals Salvation. Some churches believe that the baptism of the Holy Spirit happens to every Christian at the moment of

being born again. But the Bible says that baptism in the Holy Spirit happens after people are born again (Acts 2:1-4).

2. Necessary Sign of Tongues. Some churches believe that if someone is baptized in the Holy Spirit, he or she must speak in tongues. But the Bible says that not all believers are going to speak in tongues (1 Corinthians 12:30), even though all should be baptized in the Holy Spirit.

3. Cessationism. Some churches believe that the spiritual gifts have passed away. But the Bible never says this.

4. All Miracles are Satanic. Some churches believe that any supernatural activity today must be Satanic and can't be from God. But God is supernatural, and everything he does is supernatural.

5. All Miracles are from God. Some churches believe that all miracles are from God. But the Bible says that Satan does miracles, even in the church.

6. Spiritual Gifts are Based on Natural Abilities. Some churches believe that the natural talents of people— like helping others, administrating, or teaching— are spiritual gifts. However, people have these abilities before they are born again, showing they don't depend

on the Holy Spirit. The Bible says spiritual gifts are supernatural operations of the Holy Spirit which aren't based on human ability. A spiritual gift of teaching or helping comes from God and is supernatural. These gifts come from the Holy Spirit, only after people believe in Jesus.

7. <u>Forbidding Speaking in Tongues</u>. Some churches forbid people from speaking in tongues. But the Bible says not to forbid people from speaking in tongues (1 Corinthians 14:39).

8. <u>Tongues Must be Known Languages</u>. Some churches believe that tongues must be human languages. But the Bible says that some tongues are not understood by anyone (1 Corinthians 14:2), and might be the language of angels (1 Corinthians 13:1).

9. <u>Tongues Must Always be Understood or Interpreted</u>. Some churches believe that genuine tongues will always be understood, either by the speaker or by another hearer. But the Bible says people can speak in tongues even if no one understands them (but not in church), and that speaking in an unknown tongue edifies the speaker (1 Corinthians 14:4).

10. <u>Copying Tongues to Get the Gift of Tongues</u>. Some churches believe that if someone copies the sounds made by someone who is speaking in tongues, then he or she will get the gift of tongues. But the Bible says the gift of tongues only operates by the Holy Spirit, not by human ability.

11. <u>No Apostles or Prophets</u>. Some churches believe that the ministry positions of apostles and prophets are no longer operating in the church today. But the Bible says that these ministry gifts are needed until Christ returns (Ephesians 4:11-13).

12. <u>Prophesying Means Writing Scripture</u>. Some churches believe that prophesying is equivalent to writing Scripture and therefore there is no prophecy today. But the Bible says Agabus and Philip's daughters prophesied, but they didn't write Scripture. The New Testament commands each believer to desire to prophesy (1 Corinthians 14:1), but it's not commanding us to desire to write Scripture.

Hebrews 6:2
What are the two baptisms?

Matthew 3:11
1. Who baptizes in water?
2. Who baptizes in the Holy Spirit?

Luke 3:22, 4:1
1. Why did the Holy Spirit descend on Jesus?
2. Did Jesus have the Holy Spirit inside him before the Holy Spirit descended on him?
3. Was Jesus saved before he was baptized in water and baptized in the Holy Spirit?

Romans 8:9; 2 Corinthians 1:21-22; Ephesians 1:13-14, 4:30; 2 Corinthians 5:5
When does the Holy Spirit first indwell someone?

John 20:22
1. How do we know the disciples were born again before the Day of Pentecost?
2. How do we know the disciples had the Holy Spirit inside them before the Day of Pentecost?

Acts 1:4-8

1. What did Jesus say would be the result of being baptized in the Holy Spirit?
2. What would have happened if the disciples had begun their ministry without being baptized in the Holy Spirit?
3. Is it possible to do ministry without the baptism of the Holy Spirit?

Acts 2:1-4

1. How is the Holy Spirit like wind?
2. How is the Holy Spirit like fire?
3. What are some results of being in one accord with other believers?
4. How were the first believers baptized in the Holy Spirit?
5. Were the first disciples baptized in the Holy Spirit before or after being baptized in water?
6. Being baptized in the Holy Spirit is the same as being filled with the Holy Spirit for the first time. How is being filled with the Spirit different from being indwelt by the Holy Spirit at salvation?
7. Why do you think people often speak in tongues as a result of being baptized in the Holy Spirit?

Acts 8:12-17

1. How do we know the Samaritans were baptized in the Holy Spirit after they were born again?
2. How were the Samaritans baptized in the Holy Spirit?

Acts 9:17-18

1. Why did Jesus send Ananias to Saul?
2. How do we know Saul was a Christian before he met Ananias?
3. Was Ananias an apostle?
4. What do the scales falling from Saul's eyes symbolize about the baptism in the Holy Spirit?

Acts 10:44-48

1. How was Cornelius' household baptized in the Holy Spirit?
2. Why did Cornelius' household speak in tongues if there were no foreigners for them to preach to?

Acts 19:1-6

1. Paul called these disciples believers. What did Paul assume they believed?
2. Why did Paul ask them if they received the Holy Spirit since they believed?
3. How were they baptized in the Holy Spirit?
4. How do we know they were baptized in the Holy Spirit after being born again?
5. What are three different ways people can be baptized in the Holy Spirit according to examples in the Book of Acts?

Luke 11:11-13

1. Who was Jesus talking to, believers or unbelievers?
2. What are God's children supposed to ask God for?

3. If we pray to be baptized in the Holy Spirit, how do we know we won't receive a demon instead?

Romans 12:6-8, 1 Corinthians 12:4-11, 28, Ephesians 4:11
1. Do spiritual gifts depend on us or on God?
2. Can God work miracles? Does he?

1 Peter 4:10, Ephesians 4:16
1. Each Christian has at least one spiritual gift. Do you know what gift you have?
2. Have you ever used a spiritual gift?

1 Corinthians 14:1
Do you earnestly desire to prophesy?

1 Corinthians 14:4
What happens when someone speaks in tongues?

1 Corinthians 14:5
Why does Paul want every believer to speak in tongues?

1 Corinthians 14:18
Why do you think Paul spoke in tongues so much?

1 Corinthians 14:39
Should people be prohibited from speaking in tongues?

1 Corinthians 12:30

1. Will everyone speak in tongues?
2. Is it necessary to speak in tongues to show we have been baptized in the Holy Spirit?

1 Corinthians 13:1, 1 Corinthians 14:2

Will tongues necessarily be known languages?

1 Corinthians 14:27-28

When is it permissible to speak in tongues in church?

Acts 4:8, 4:31, 7:55, 13:9, 13:52; Ephesians 5:18

Who needs to be filled with the Holy Spirit?
Why are Christians commanded to be filled with the Holy Spirit?

Have you ever been baptized in the Holy Spirit? If so, when?

5

Laying on of Hands

THE FIFTH FOUNDATIONAL PRINCIPLE of Jesus Christ is the laying on of hands. The laying on of hands is a spiritual tool that can release the power of God into people's lives.

Throughout his ministry, Jesus laid hands on people.

"Then little children were brought to Him that He might put His hands on them and pray... and He laid His hands on them" (Matt. 19:13-15). Jesus blessed these children. "And He took them up in His arms, laid His hands on them, and blessed them" (Mark 10:16).

Jesus laid hands on the sick to heal them. One day a leper came to Jesus and asked if he was willing to heal him.

"Then Jesus put out His hand and touched him, saying, 'I am willing; be cleansed.' Immediately his leprosy was cleansed" (Matthew 8:3).

After this, Jesus went into Peter's house.

"Now when Jesus had come into Peter's house, He saw his wife's mother lying sick with a fever. So He touched her hand, and the fever left her" (Matthew 8:14-15a).

In the evening of the same day, Jesus healed many people.

> When evening had come, they brought to Him many who were demon-possessed. And He cast out the spirits with a word, and healed all who were sick, that it might be fulfilled which was spoken by Isaiah the prophet, saying: "He Himself took our infirmities and bore our sicknesses." (Matthew 8:16-17)

Jesus healed *all* who were sick in Capernaum. Luke tells us they were healed through the laying on of hands.

> When the sun was setting, all those who had any that were sick with various diseases brought them to Him;

and He laid His hands on every one of them and healed them. (Luke 4:40)

When Jesus laid hands on people, he released spiritual power. This spiritual power brought physical transformation to heal sick bodies.

Healing Brought by Jesus

Jesus' healing miracles fulfilled a prophecy from Isaiah chapter 53, quoted in Matthew 8:17.

Surely He has borne our griefs and carried our sorrows; yet we esteemed Him stricken, smitten by God, and afflicted. But He was wounded for our transgressions, He was bruised for our iniquities; the chastisement for our peace was upon Him, and by His stripes we are healed. (Isaiah 53:4-5)

Around 700 BC, Isaiah prophesied that Christ would die for the sins of the world. All our sins would be laid upon him, God's wrath would fall upon him, and he would die in our place. In this way, he would take away our sins and all the evil results of sin.

Isaiah 53:4 says that Christ would take our *griefs* and *sorrows* (NKJV). These Hebrew words, *choli* and *makob*, refer to sicknesses and diseases. The apostle Matthew, quoting this same verse from Isaiah, translates these words as *infirmities* and *sicknesses* (Matt. 8:17). This is the correct translation, given by God himself by the inspiration of the Holy Spirit.

The Hebrew word *choli*, used 24 times in the Old Testament, is almost always translated *sickness* or *disease*. It ought to be translated as such in Isa. 53:4. The Hebrew word *makob* occurs 16 times in the Old Testament. This word can be translated as either *pain* or *sorrow*. Matthew, through his Greek translation, confirms that these Hebrew words refer to physical sicknesses.

Christ's redemption is complete. His blood is sufficient to resolve all evil that humanity faces, including sickness, disease, pain, sorrow, or depression. Everything can be healed by Christ, because he took sin away. With the root of evil gone, sin's branches will all fall down.

Appropriating the Victory of Christ

Someone might say, "Wait a minute. If Jesus came to take away our sicknesses, then why do we still get sick?"

This can be answered by asking another question: If Jesus died on the cross for our sins, then why do we still sin?

Jesus paid the price to take all our sins away, but we're not yet experiencing the full victory over sin. In the same way, Jesus is able to take all our sicknesses away, but we still get sick. But as we grow spiritually, we will experience increasing victory over sin and all its evil results in our lives.

When we get sick, we don't need to be overwhelmed. There is victory in Christ, and he can heal us. But even if we don't experience victory the way we would like, God is so powerful that he can bring some kind of good out of any kind of evil.

"And we know that all things work together for good to those who love God, to those who are the called according to His purpose" (Romans 8:28).

The Disciples Lay Hands on the Sick

Jesus healed the sick through the laying on of hands, and he commanded his disciples to heal the sick through the laying on of hands.

"And as you go, preach, saying, 'The kingdom of heaven is at hand.' Heal the sick" (Matthew 10:7-8a).

"Lay hands on the sick, and they will recover" (Mark 16:18b).

Miraculous healings are part of the growth of the kingdom of God upon the earth.

"Most assuredly, I say to you, he who believes in Me, the works that I do he will do also; and greater works than these he will do, because I go to My Father" (John 14:12).

Throughout the book of Acts, believers laid hands on sick people and healed them.

"The father of Publius lay sick of a fever and dysentery. Paul went in to him and prayed, and he laid his hands on him and healed him" (Acts 28:8).

Laying on of Hands for Fellowship

The laying on of hands reveals the importance of the body of Christ. It shows that we need each other in order to grow spiritually. Saul, who became Paul, met Jesus on the Damascus road, and his life was transformed. But Saul needed more than a revelation of Jesus to fulfill his calling. He also needed a revelation of the body of Christ. That's why God sent a brother named Ananias to lay hands on him. Nothing else is said in the Bible about Ananias. But Ananias was important because he represented the body of Christ to Saul. When Ananias laid hands on Saul, his eyes were healed, and he was filled with the Holy Spirit.

The laying on of hands reminds us that God's power is within his people, and that none of us can accomplish God's plans apart from the church. We are not called to live the Christian life as individuals. We need each other to reach our full potential in God.

"For as the body is one and has many members, but all the members of that one body, being many, are one body, so also is Christ" (1 Corinthians 12:12).

The laying on of hands is a sign that we are connected to our brothers and sisters in the family of God. When one believer lays hands on another by the leading of God, the spiritual power within the body of Christ operates.

God's Church Pattern

The laying on of hands is a special ministry of the church. In order to understand this ministry, we must first understand church.

Church is not a building. Neither Jesus nor his apostles told anyone to build a "church" building, and for the first three centuries of Christianity, not one such building was constructed. Church is not a denomination. Jesus prayed that all his disciples would be one (John 17:21), and Paul specifically forbade the creation of denominations (1 Corinthians 1:11-13).

The most basic expression of church in the New Testament is the house church. House churches are mentioned in Acts 2:46, Romans 16:3-5, 1 Corinthians 16:19, Colossians 4:15, Philemon 2, and in other verses. In house churches, believers met together regularly, ate common meals, supported each other, and had participatory meetings.

In the New Testament, all the house churches in a city were part of the church in that city. In each city there were possibly hundreds of believers, and these believers were part of different house churches scattered throughout each city. (See for example Romans 16:5,14,15.)

All Christians all over the world are part of the church all over the world. This vast worldwide church is the body of Christ.

We need to understand God's definition of church if we are going to be part of church as God intends. We are under no obligation to be a part of church as defined by man. But we are obligated to be part of church as defined by God. It is within the church that laying on of hands will operate.

Laying on of Hands for the Baptism of the Holy Spirit

The laying on of hands can spark the baptism in the Holy Spirit.

When Ananias laid hands on Saul, he was baptized in the Holy Spirit.

In Ephesus, Paul laid hands on believers and they were baptized in the Holy Spirit. "When Paul had laid hands on them, the Holy Spirit came upon them, and they spoke with tongues and prophesied" (Acts 19:6).

In Samaria, believers were baptized in the Holy Spirit through the laying on of hands.

> Then they laid hands on them, and they received the Holy Spirit. And when Simon saw that through the laying on of the apostles' hands the Holy Spirit was given, he offered them money, saying, "Give me this power also, that anyone on whom I lay hands may receive the Holy Spirit." (Acts 8:17-19)

A man named Simon saw that through the laying on of hands people were baptized in the Holy Spirit. He wanted the same power. Peter rebuked him, saying that this power was a "gift from God." The power of the laying on of hands is not something that operates by human will or power, but according to the Holy Spirit.

Laying on of Hands to Impart Spiritual Gifts

The laying on of hands can impart spiritual gifts. A group of elders once laid hands on Timothy to impart to him a spiritual gift. Paul advised Timothy, "Do not neglect the gift that is in you, which was given to you by prophecy with the laying on of the hands of the eldership" (1 Timothy 4:14).

Timothy also received a spiritual gift when Paul laid hands on him. "Therefore I remind you to stir up the gift of God which is in you through the laying on of my hands" (2 Timothy 1:6).

When the Holy Spirit reveals that God wants to equip someone with a spiritual gift, that gift can be imparted through the laying on of hands.

Laying on of Hands to Commission for Ministry

The laying on of hands can set people apart for new ministry. When Stephen and other men were chosen to do ministry in the early church, the apostles laid hands on them - "whom they set before the apostles; and when they had prayed, they laid hands on them" (Acts 6:6). The laying on of hands separated these men for their new service to God.

Five prophets and teachers were at the church in Antioch. When two of them, Paul and Barnabas, were about to become apostles, the others laid hands on them.

> As they ministered to the Lord and fasted, the Holy Spirit said, "Now separate to Me Barnabas and Saul for the work to which I have called them." Then, having fasted and prayed, and laid hands on them, they sent them away. (Acts 13:2-3)

The laying on of hands marked the point at which Barnabas and Saul were elevated from being prophets or teachers to being apostles. The laying on of hands imparted spiritual power which elevated them to this new level of service.

Don't Lay Hands Quickly

Laying on of hands must be done by the leading of the Holy Spirit.

"Don't lay hands too quickly on anyone, neither be partaker of other people's sins. Keep yourself pure" (1 Timothy 5:22).

Don't lay hands quickly on anyone, either imparting to them spiritual gifts or ordaining them for ministry. Placing someone into a ministry position too quickly will cause problems for the church. Paul gives the following advice when ordaining deacons: "But let these also first be tested; then let them serve as deacons, being found blameless" (1 Timothy 3:10). People must prove their character before being put into leadership positions.

The laying on of hands is a way to impart blessing from God. It can heal the sick, spark the baptism of the Holy Spirit, impart spiritual gifts, and launch someone into a new ministry. The laying on of hands is a powerful ministry of the church, and it is a means through which the power of Christ operates within his body. It is the fifth foundational principle of Jesus Christ.

~ *Prayer* ~

Dear God, thank you for the spiritual power that can be released through the laying on of hands. You want your people to heal the sick through the laying on of hands. You desire to baptize people in the Holy Spirit and impart spiritual gifts through the laying on of hands. Lead me by your Spirit so I know when you want me to lay hands on someone, and when you want someone to lay hands on me. Help me to understand church as you define church, so that

I may experience her power in the way you intend. Connect me to like-minded believers, who will seek to follow you the way your word instructs. And let your Holy Spirit work powerfully among your people as they submit to your will. In Jesus' name I pray. Amen.

Victory Over False Teachings

1. <u>Clergy Must Lay Hands</u>. Some churches believe that only professional priests or clergy should lay hands on people. But the Bible says the laying on of hands can be done by any believer who is led by God to do so.

2. <u>No Healing From God</u>. Some churches teach that God does not heal people supernaturally today, and that sickness when it happens is God's will. But the Bible says Jesus healed every sick person who came to him while he walked the earth. Jesus commanded his disciples to heal the sick too, giving them spiritual power to do so.

3. <u>No Sickness</u>. Some churches believe that true Christians will never get sick. But the Bible says complete freedom from all sickness will only occur at the end of the age (Revelation 21:4).

4. Everyone Will Be Healed. Some churches teach that we should pray indiscriminately for everyone to be healed, and they will be. But the Bible says we need to be led by the Holy Spirit in our ministry (Luke 4:25-27).

5. No Medicine. Some churches condemn all use of medicine. But the Bible doesn't (1 Timothy 5:23).

6. Church is a Building. Some churches say that churches are buildings, and that we should build "church" buildings. But the Bible says church is a people, and it nowhere tells anyone to build a "church" building. The early church met in homes.

7. Church is a Denomination. Some churches say that each congregation should be part of a denomination. But the Bible forbids denominations (1 Corinthians 1:12). Jesus prayed that all his people would be one (John 17:21). The divisions of the church in the New Testament were purely geographic.

8. Seminary is Required. Some churches believe that if someone wants to become a minister, he must go to seminary. But there were no seminaries in the New Testament, yet there were plenty of effective minis-

ters. The Bible says that to serve God, we must be called and equipped by God himself (1 John 2:27).

Matthew 19:13-15, Mark 10:16

1. Why were these children blessed when Jesus laid hands on them?
2. Why didn't Jesus just speak a blessing to these children instead of laying hands on them?
3. How can blessings and curses affect our lives?

Matthew 8:14-15, Luke 4:40

Why does God choose to heal people through the laying on of hands?

Matthew 8:16-17, Isaiah 53:4-6

1. Where does sickness come from? Is sickness from God?
2. Why did Jesus' death on the cross take away our sicknesses?
3. Why do we still get sick?
4. If Jesus died to take away our sins, why do we still sin?
5. How do we experience more victory over sin?
6. Can we experience increasing victory over sickness?

Romans 8:28

1. How does God bring good out of sickness or other bad events?

2. Have you ever experienced God bringing good out of something bad?

Matthew 10:7-8, John 14:12, Mark 16:18, Acts 28:8

1. Can you work miracles?
2. Have you ever done a miracle?
3. Have you ever laid hands on a sick person and prayed for him to recover? What happened?
4. Have you ever been miraculously healed?

Acts 2:46, Romans 16:3-5, 1 Corinthians 16:19, Colossians 4:15, Philemon 2

1. Why did the early church meet in house churches?
2. Are there any examples of church buildings in the New Testament?
3. Does God recognize city church today like he did in the New Testament?
4. Were there denominations in the New Testament?
5. How does laying on of hands reveal the importance of the church?

Acts 8:17-19, Acts 19:6

Why does God baptize people in the Holy Spirit through the laying on of hands?

1 Timothy 4:14, 2 Timothy 1:6

Why does God impart spiritual gifts through the laying on of hands?

Acts 6:6, Acts 13:2-3, Acts 14:4

1. Why did the apostles lay hands on those who had been chosen to be ministers?
2. What ministry did Paul and Barnabas have before the brethren in Antioch laid hands on them? What ministry did they have after this?

1 Timothy 5:22

1. Why shouldn't we lay hands quickly on someone?
2. How can laying hands on someone too quickly defile us?
3. Is it possible to be spiritually defiled when someone lays hands on us?

6

Resurrection of the Dead

THE SIXTH FOUNDATIONAL TEACHING of Jesus is the resurrection of the dead. Resurrection is a promise of living forever with God.

People all over the world want to live forever. Throughout history, people have followed religious rituals, hoping to gain eternal life. Ancient explorers sought a fountain of life from which they hoped to get immortality. Today, Silicon Valley corporate leaders are trying to extend the human life span through advances in medicine, robotics, and artificial intelligence.

All these human attempts to find immortality are doomed to failure. There is only one way to get eternal life - as a gift from God. And the only way to receive this gift is to believe in Jesus Christ.

"I am the resurrection and the life; he who believes in Me will live even if he dies" (John 11:25).

The fundamental problem we have is not disease or aging. It is sin. Sin separates humanity from God, and it ultimately kills. The only way our sins can be cleansed is through faith in Jesus Christ.

Spiritual Resurrection

When we are born again, we are spiritually resurrected along with Jesus.

We are "raised with [Jesus] through faith in the working of God, who raised Him from the dead" (Colossians 2:12).

Jesus rose from the dead, and the resurrection power of Jesus Christ operates inside each child of God. We need to know this stupendous power - "the exceeding greatness of His power toward us who believe, according to the working of His mighty power which He worked in Christ when He raised Him from the dead and seated Him at His right hand in the heavenly places" (Ephesians 1:19-20).

The resurrection power of Jesus is the power to save our souls, and this power is to affect every aspect of our lives, including our physical bodies.

> But if the Spirit of Him who raised Jesus from the dead dwells in you, He who raised Christ from the dead will also give life to your mortal bodies through His Spirit who dwells in you. (Romans 8:11)

Living by Resurrection Power

We are called to live by this awesome resurrection power.

"Just as Christ was raised from the dead by the glory of the Father, even so we also should walk in newness of life" (Romans 6:4).

Walking in "newness of life" means walking by the Holy Spirit. We are not to live according to the flesh (our own wisdom, power, and righteousness), but according to the Holy Spirit (the wisdom, power, and righteousness of Christ). The Christian life is supernatural, above our natural abilities. It depends on God's power, not our own power.

"Therefore, if anyone is in Christ, he is a new creation; old things have passed away; behold, all things have become new" (2 Corinthians 5:17).

To experience this newness, we need to "know Christ and the power of his resurrection" (Philippians 3:10). As we increasingly know Jesus and the power of his resurrection, we will increasingly experience God's power working within us and through us.

Eternal Souls

Because of the resurrection of Jesus, we already have eternal life now.

"For God so loved the world that He gave His only begotten Son, that whoever believes in Him should not perish but have everlasting life" (John 3:16).

Our souls became eternally alive the moment we were born again. We don't need to fear death because even if our bodies perish, our souls will go to heaven. Nothing can really kill us. We have victory in life, and we have victory in death.

"To die is gain... [I] desire to depart and be with Christ, which is far better" (Philippians 1:21-23).

Where do we go when we die? When our bodies die, our souls will immediately go to be with Christ.

"To be absent from the body is to be present with the Lord" (2 Corinthians 5:8).

And when we are in heaven with Christ, we will be spiritually more alive than ever.

Dead People Cannot Interact with the Earth

When our bodies die, our souls will go to be with God, and that is something to look forward to. But we have a job to do on the earth, revealing the gospel to the world and building the church. That's why Paul wanted to go to be with God, but he said, "to remain in the flesh is more needful for you" (Philippians 1:24). Although Paul wanted to go to heaven and enjoy God's direct presence, he knew he was called to stay in his physical body so he could keep serving the church. He knew that without a physical body, he would be unable to help anyone on the earth.

The New Testament describes the death of Christians as *falling asleep*.

> But I do not want you to be ignorant, brethren, concerning those who have fallen asleep, lest you sorrow as others who have no hope. For if we believe that Jesus died and rose again, even so God will bring with Him those who sleep in Jesus. (1 Thessalonians 4:13-14)

Sleeping refers to the relationship that dead saints have with the world. Dead saints can't do anything on the earth. They can't speak to anyone or appear to anyone.

They can't interact with us or help us in any way. Although they are more alive and conscious of God than ever before, as pertaining to the world, they are asleep.

No dead saint can help us relate to God or get anything from God. Dead saints cannot answer our prayers. It's impossible to communicate with them. No dead person can interact with us. The souls of dead people are either in heaven or in hell; there is no middle ground. Jesus is the only mediator between us and God. "For there is one God and one Mediator between God and men, the Man Christ Jesus" (1 Timothy 2:5).

Supposed interactions with the dead are often imaginary, but they could be demonic. Any spirit that claims to be a dead person is a lying spirit - either a demon or a fallen angel. Satan often lies and pretends to be someone he's not (2 Corinthians 11:14). We should never seek to hear from any dead person or accept any communications from "dead" people. This will open the door to the devil. We need to hear from God alone.

The only way dead saints can interact with the world is for them to be physically resurrected.

Resurrection of the Mortal Body

Several people have been physically resurrected in the Bible.

Elijah prayed for a dead boy, and his soul came back into his body by the power of God (1 Kings 17:17-24).

Elisha raised up a dead boy (2 Kings 4:18-37).

Jesus raised up a dead boy (Luke 7:11-17). He also raised a girl back to life (Luke 8:52-56). He raised Lazarus up from the dead (John 11).

Peter raised up Dorcas from the dead (Acts 9:36-43).

Resurrections happen today in hospitals. Some people clinically die and then come back to life. Resurrections can also happen today through the power of God. When Jesus sent his disciples out to do ministry, he commanded them to raise the dead (Matthew 10:8a). It is possible to raise the dead by God's power, according to the leading of God's Spirit.

What happened to all these people who were resurrected? Everyone who has ever been physically resurrected, whether medically or miraculously, died again because they were resurrected in their mortal bodies. All except one man.

The Resurrection of Jesus Christ

Jesus' resurrection is the greatest resurrection of all. When other people died, they died for their own sins, but when Jesus died, he died for the sins of the whole world. He "tasted death for everyone" (Hebrews 2:9). But even all these sins couldn't hold him down. He resurrected, defeating all sin.

The resurrection of Jesus is the dynamo of Christianity. Without it, our faith would be totally empty, devoid of power.

"And if Christ is not risen, then our preaching is empty and your faith is also empty" (1 Corinthians 15:14).

But Christ did rise from the dead, meaning our faith is full of death-destroying power. He crushed Satan's head, demolished sin, and set us free from death.

Glorified Bodies

At the end of the age, all believers will be physically resurrected. Our souls will receive glorified bodies which will last forever.

"For we know that if the earthly tent which is our house is torn down, we have a building from God, a house not made with hands, eternal in the heavens" (2 Corinthians 5:1).

Job said, "And after my skin is destroyed, this I know, that in my flesh I shall see God" (Job 19:26).

Isaiah said, "Your dead shall live; together with my dead body, they shall arise. Awake and sing, you who dwell in dust; for your dew is like the dew of herbs" (Isaiah 26:19).

God told Daniel, "But as for you, go your way to the end; then you will enter into rest and rise again for your allotted portion at the end of the age" (Daniel 12:13).

The promise of future resurrection in a glorified body is worth looking forward to.

Levels of Eternal Glory

After the resurrection, the glorified bodies of the saints will be bright with God's glory. Some glorified bodies will be brighter than others.

> There is one glory of the sun, another glory of the moon, and another glory of the stars; for one star differs from another star in glory. So also is the resurrection of the dead. (1 Corinthians 15:41-42a)

Christ will give heavenly rewards to his people based on their level of obedience to him while living on the earth. Based on the amount of rewards received, each one will shine forth glory throughout eternity.

Jesus told his disciples, "Lay up for yourselves treasures in heaven" (Matthew 6:20). We lay up treasure in heaven as we obey God and make sacrifices for him on this earth. Our glorified bodies will reflect the amount of heavenly treasure we have in eternity.

Paul said the challenges he endured for the sake of Jesus created for him a more glorious eternal future. "For our light affliction, which is but for a moment, is working for us a far more exceeding and eternal weight of glory" (2 Corinthians 4:17). As Paul took up his cross and followed Christ, he was laying up heavenly treasure. This weight of glory would be revealed in his glorified body.

Changed Into Glory At the Last Trumpet

At the end of the age, some believers will get their glorified bodies while they are still alive.

> We shall not all sleep, but we shall all be changed - in a moment, in the twinkling of an eye, at the last trumpet. For the trumpet will sound, and the dead will be

raised incorruptible, and we shall be changed. (1 Corinthians 15:51b-52)

When Christ returns to the earth, the living saints will be transformed from mortal to immortal. How awesome would that be!

At the resurrection, the living saints will put on glorified bodies.

> "[God] will transform our lowly body that it may be conformed to His glorious body, according to the working by which He is able even to subdue all things to Himself" (Philippians 3:21).

> We who are alive and remain until the coming of the Lord will by no means precede those who are asleep. For the Lord Himself will descend from heaven with a shout, with the voice of an archangel, and with the trumpet of God. And the dead in Christ will rise first. Then we who are alive and remain shall be caught up together with them in the clouds to meet the Lord in the air. And thus we shall always be with the Lord. Therefore comfort one another with these words. (1 Thessalonians 4:15b-17)

At the last trumpet, three things will happen:

1. Jesus will return to the earth.
2. The dead in Christ will be resurrected.
3. The living saints will put on their glorified bodies.

There are 7 final trumpets listed in Revelation, and the last trumpet is the 7th.

> In the days of the sounding of the seventh angel, when he is about to [trumpet], the mystery of God would be finished, as He declared to His servants the prophets. (Revelation 10:7)

The last trumpet marks the end of the age. When it sounds, there will be no more time (Revelation 10:6).

We are spiritually resurrected now through faith in God, and our souls have become eternally alive. We are called to live on the earth by the power of Christ's resurrection. A few people are resurrected now on earth in their mortal bodies, but they die again. At the last trumpet, all the saints will be resurrected physically, and the believers who are alive on the earth will put on glorified bodies. Understanding these things about the resurrection of the dead is the sixth foundational principle of Jesus Christ.

~ *Prayer* ~

Heavenly Father, praise you for the power of resurrection. When Jesus rose up from the dead, he conquered every enemy, including sin and death. The power of resurrection is at work in my life because the Holy Spirit is inside me. Help me to see this! Help me experience it! I want to live the supernatural life that you intended me to live. I'm tired of living a mundane life. Release me from every bondage. Heal my body and give me spiritual strength to do what you want me to do. In Jesus' name I pray. Amen.

Victory Over False Teachings

1. <u>Soul Sleep</u>. Some churches believe that the souls of Christians will fall asleep at death and only become conscious again at the resurrection. But the Bible says that to depart from the body is to be present with the Lord, and this is a conscious reality (Philippians 1:23). Although dead saints are asleep as pertaining to the world, they are very much alive and awake to God.

2. <u>Living Saints Will be Raptured Before Trumpet 7</u>. Some churches believe that the church will be raptured before the 7th trumpet. But the Bible says that the dead saints will be resurrected, the living saints will be transformed, and the events of 1 Thessalonians

4:15-17 will all occur at the last trumpet (compare 1 Corinthians 15:51-52).

John 11:25
Why is it impossible to get eternal life apart from Jesus?

John 3:16
How do people get eternal life?

John 17:3
What is eternal life?

Colossians 2:12
How are believers already raised from the dead?

Romans 8:11
How should the resurrection of Jesus affect our bodies?

Romans 6:4, 2 Corinthians 5:17
1. What does it mean to walk in newness of life?
2. How do we walk in newness of life?

Philippians 3:10
What is some evidence of the resurrection power of Christ operating in our lives?

Philippians 1:21-23, 2 Corinthians 5:8
1. When a believer dies, what happens to his soul?

2. Why should Christians be unafraid of death?

Philippians 1:24, 1 Thessalonians 4:13-14

1. Why would Paul be unable to help the church if his body was dead?
2. Can dead people interact with living people?
3. Where do people go when they die?

1 Timothy 2:5

1. Why are dead saints unable to answer our prayers?
2. Should we say, "Hail Mary"?
3. When people claim to talk to dead people, who are they talking to?

Job 19:26, Isaiah 26:19, Daniel 12:13

How does the doctrine of resurrection encourage those who go through challenges?

1 Kings 17:17-24, 2 Kings 4:18-37, 2 Kings 13:21

Why did these resurrected people die again?

Luke 7:11-17, Luke 8:52-56, John 11, Acts 9:36-43, Acts 20:7-12, Matt. 27:50-53

1. What is the difference between the resurrection of Jesus Christ and the resurrection of everyone else?
2. What did the resurrection of Jesus accomplish?

1 Corinthians 15:14

Why is Christianity powerless without the resurrection of Jesus?

Matthew 10:8

1. Is it possible to raise the dead today?
2. Do you know anyone who has ever been resurrected - either medically or through God's power?

2 Corinthians 5:1

Why is the body like a tent?

1 Corinthians 15:41-42

How will different levels of glory be revealed in eternity?

2 Corinthians 4:17, 2 Corinthians 5:10, Matthew 6:20

What are some ways we can lay up spiritual treasure in heaven?

1 Corinthians 15:51-52, 1 Thessalonians 4:15-17, Revelation 10:6

What three main events will happen at the last trumpet? How does this affect your view of the end times?

7

Eternal Judgment

ETERNAL JUDGMENT is the seventh and final foundational doctrine of Christ.

God is the great judge. At the end of time, he will judge everyone. Both believers and unbelievers will stand before his throne. Everyone who ever lived, from the beginning of time until the end of time, will be there.

> Then I saw a great white throne and Him who sat on it, from whose face the earth and the heaven fled away. And there was found no place for them. And I saw the dead, small and great, standing before God,

and books were opened. And another book was opened, which is the Book of Life. And the dead were judged according to their works, by the things which were written in the books. (Revelation 20:11-12)

All our works are being recorded in books by God. At the end of time, these books will be opened. Everything about our lives will be laid bare, and we will have no secrets.

Today, when people are asked how they will get into heaven, they often reply, "Because I'm a good person." But our works, no matter how good, will never get us into heaven. The only way we can get to heaven is if our names are written in the Book of Life. Our names are inscribed in the book of life when we trust in Jesus Christ alone for salvation.

At the judgment, the Book of Life (Revelation 20:11) will determine our eternal destination— heaven or hell. The other heavenly books which record our works (Revelation 20:12) will determine our levels within heaven or hell.

Before the Throne of God

There are only two possible destinations for every person's soul after death: heaven or hell.

"It is appointed for men to die once, but after this the judgment" (Hebrews 9:27).

There is no middle ground. There is no place like purgatory, where people pay for their sins and then get out. There is no way anyone can pay for their sins. Sin is an infinite affront to God, and it would take an eternity to pay for it. The blood of Christ alone can pay for sin.

At the final judgment, every person who ever lived, from the beginning of time until the end of time, will be separated into two groups.

> When the Son of Man comes in His glory, and all the holy angels with Him, then He will sit on the throne of His glory. All the nations will be gathered before Him, and He will separate them one from another, as a shepherd divides his sheep from the goats. And He will set the sheep on His right hand, but the goats on the left. (Matthew 25:31-33)

Sheep symbolize those who believe in Jesus. Goats symbolize those who don't.

Jesus said,

> Do not marvel at this; for the hour is coming in which all who are in the graves will hear His voice and come

forth—those who have done good, to the resurrection of life, and those who have done evil, to the resurrection of condemnation. (John 5:28-29)

At the end of the age, those who have "done good" will be resurrected into glorified bodies. The "good" they have done is trusted in Jesus.

"What shall we do, that we may work the works of God?" Jesus answered and said to them, "This is the work of God, that you believe in Him whom He sent." (John 6:28-29)

Those who never trusted in Christ will be part of the "resurrection of condemnation." At this resurrection, the souls of unbelievers will be united with bodies of darkness, and they will be thrown into the lake of fire.

"Fear [God] who is able to destroy both soul and body in hell" (Matthew 10:28b).

Hell is a place where both soul *and* body will experience eternal destruction.

Heaven and Hell Are Forever

The judgment of God is eternal. In Greek, the word for *eternity* is αἰώνιον (aionion). This same Greek word describes the duration of life in heaven and the duration of punishment in hell.

"And these [unbelievers] will go away into everlasting [αἰώνιον] punishment, but the righteous into eternal [αἰώνιον] life" (Matthew 25:46).

Heaven is forever. Eternal life means consciously enjoying God's presence, forever.

"For God so loved the world that He gave His only begotten Son, that whoever believes in Him should not perish but have everlasting [αἰώνιον] life" (John 3:16).

Jesus also said, "I give them eternal [αἰώνιον] life" (John 10:28).

Hell is also forever. The same Greek word that describes the duration of the afterlife in heaven, also describes the duration of the afterlife in hell.

"It is better for you to enter into life lame or maimed, rather than having two hands or two feet, to be cast into the everlasting [αἰώνιον] fire" (Matthew 18:8).

"These shall be punished with everlasting [αἰώνιον] destruction from the presence of the Lord and from the glory of His power" (2 Thessalonians 1:9).

In the Old Testament, Daniel used the Hebrew word *olam* to describe the duration of the afterlife, both for the righteous and for the wicked. *Olam* means *eternal, forever*.

> And many of those who sleep in the dust of the earth shall awake, some to everlasting [*olam*] life, some to shame and everlasting [*olam*] contempt. Those who are wise shall shine like the brightness of the firmament, and those who turn many to righteousness like the stars forever and ever. (Daniel 12:2-3)

The eternal state is permanent. There will be no departure from heaven for the righteous and no escape from hell for the wicked.

The Reason for Eternal Hell

Hell is eternal because God is infinitely valuable. To reject God is to reject everything that is good. This terrible choice has disastrous consequences. People who reject God often don't face the consequences of this choice while living on the earth, because God waits patiently for them to turn to him. But when they die, they will have no more chance to accept God.

Jesus paid an infinite price to reconcile us to an infinitely good God. If we refuse the infinitely valuable gift of God's

Son, we make an infinitely bad decision. And the penalty for rejecting infinite good is infinite evil.

What Hell is Like

Jesus talked a lot about hell. He described it as a "fire that shall never be quenched" (Mark 9:44a). Fire burns and causes pain. It consumes and destroys. The fire of hell can never be quenched. It will never go out. It will burn forever.

In hell, worms will eat away at the damned. Jesus said that in hell "their worm does not die and the fire is not quenched" (Mark 9:44b). This word *worm* could also be translated as gnawing anguish. The anguish of hell is never-ending.

Hell is a place of conscious torment. When a man died and his soul went into hell, he cried out, "I am tormented in this flame!" (Luke 16:24b). The man was conscious and in pain, as he crackled and burned in hell.

Hell is a furnace of fire.

> The angels will come forth, separate the wicked from among the just, and cast them into the furnace of fire. There will be wailing and gnashing of teeth. (Matthew 13:50)

> ...as Sodom and Gomorrah, and the cities around them in a similar manner to these, having given themselves over to sexual immorality and gone after strange flesh, are set forth as an example, suffering the vengeance of eternal [αἰώνιον] fire. (Jude 7)

The people who lived in the cities of Sodom and Gomorrah are currently suffering the vengeance of God in hell-fire. This vengeance is eternal.

Hell is a spiritual fire where souls will weep and wail in excruciating pain. The sounds of screaming will be all around. Souls will figuratively gnash their teeth with remorse, regret, guilt, and shame.

Hell does not erase people so they no longer exist. Hell torments them.

"And the smoke of their torment ascends forever and ever; and they have no rest day or night" (Revelation 14:11a).

Those who are in hell will never get any rest. Their exhaustion and pain will be eternal.

Hell is a lake of fire. "And anyone not found written in the Book of Life was cast into the lake of fire" (Rev. 20:15). All those who are not born again will be thrown into this lake of fire.

But the cowardly, unbelieving, abominable, murderers, sexually immoral, sorcerers, idolaters, and all liars shall have their part in the lake which burns with fire and brimstone, which is the second death. (Revelation 21:8)

Brimstone is an ancient word for sulfur. When sulfur burns, it becomes a sticky liquid that smells like rotten eggs. If the smoke of burning sulfur comes into contact with any moisture, it produces toxic gas. If a person breathes this gas, it forms a deadly acid inside their lungs which chokes them and burns them on the inside. This causes suffocation.

When unbelievers die, their souls immediately go into hell where they begin to suffer. They will choke, burn, and be in unimaginable pain.

Jesus told about a rich man who died and immediately went into hell.

And being in torments in Hades, he lifted up his eyes and saw Abraham afar off, and Lazarus in his bosom. Then he cried and said, "Father Abraham, have mercy on me, and send Lazarus that he may dip the tip of his finger in water and cool my tongue; for I am tormented in this flame." (Luke 16:23-24)

People in hell will die eternally. They will experience the pain of death forever. Hell is the worst nightmare anyone could imagine.

On earth there are some good things and some bad things. But eternity will be extremes. In heaven there will be no bad things. In hell there will be no good things.

Just as there are levels of rewards in heaven, so there will be levels of punishment in hell. Jesus told some who rejected the gospel that "it will be more tolerable for Tyre and Sidon at the judgment than for you" (Luke 10:14). The torment in hell for those who reject Jesus will be worse than the torment of the people who lived in the wicked cities of Tyre and Sidon. Those who reject Jesus had an opportunity to trust in him for salvation, but those in Tyre and Sidon never had such an opportunity.

Motivated to Evangelize

Who can tolerate the thought of their friends and family members burning forever in hell? The thought is terrible.

If someone knows the cure for a deadly disease but withholds treatment, he is guilty. In the same way, if we know that people without Christ are heading into hell and we don't share the gospel with them, we are guilty. We need to share the gospel with unbelievers so they don't end up in hell.

"Knowing, therefore, the terror of the Lord, we persuade men" (2 Corinthians 5:11a).

God can use the terrors of hell to save people. People will be reached with the gospel in different ways. We need to be led by the Holy Spirit in order to know how to share the gospel with each person. Some people will be saved when we show them compassion, while others will be saved when they are struck by the terrors of hell.

"And on some have compassion, making a distinction; but others save with fear, pulling them out of the fire, hating even the garment defiled by the flesh" (Jude 22-23).

Judgment of Christians

Christians are free from hell by the blood of Jesus. Praise God for the infinite power of Christ's blood. Although they are eternally safe, Christians will still be judged by God.

"So then each of us shall give account of himself to God" (Romans 14:12).

We will give account to God for our words. "But I say to you that for every idle word men may speak, they will give account of it in the day of judgment" (Matthew 12:36).

We will also give an account for our actions:

> We must all appear before the judgment seat of Christ, that each one may receive the things done in the body, according to what he has done, whether good or bad. (2 Corinthians 5:9-10)

When we are judged by God, we will receive rewards based on how we lived on the earth.

> Now if anyone builds on this foundation with gold, silver, precious stones, wood, hay, straw, each one's work will become clear; for the Day will declare it, because it will be revealed by fire; and the fire will test each one's work, of what sort it is. If anyone's work which he has built on it endures, he will receive a reward. If anyone's work is burned, he will suffer loss; but he himself will be saved, yet so as through fire. (2 Corinthians 3:12-15)

The foundation for everything good in the world is Jesus Christ. More specifically, the foundation of the church is Jesus Christ. He is the chief cornerstone for this great house of God on the earth, comprised of everyone who believes in Jesus. If something is built on the foundation of Jesus that is according to God, it will remain. If something is built that is not according to God, it will be destroyed. Only the things that we do in this life that are according to the word of God will last forever. Whatever we do that is not according to the word of God will lack eternal value and be destroyed. Believers will all be saved; yet they will go through a fire that will test all their works. This is connected to judgment, the seventh foundational principle of Jesus Christ.

As long as we are on the earth, we need to live in the light of God's throne and make the most of our lives. Whatever we do now has eternal consequences. Let's make wise use of our days and invest our time and energy for eternity.

This begins with understanding and implementing the seven basic doctrines of Jesus Christ.

~ *Prayer* ~

Dear God, I am only on this earth for a short time. Eternity is vast in comparison. Help me to live in the blazing light of eternity. Give me wisdom and power to speak your gospel to those who don't know you. You don't want anyone to perish, and I don't either. Help me to be an agent of your salvation. Cause the reality of hell to motivate me to evangelize. I know that someday I will stand before your throne, and you will judge me. Thank you for the precious blood of your Son, which cleanses me from all sin. Help me to do things of eternal value and stop wasting my life with things that don't matter. In Jesus' name, I pray. Amen.

Victory Over False Teachings

1. <u>Universal Reconciliation</u>. Some churches believe that everyone will ultimately be saved and reconciled to God. But the Bible says that many people are going to end up in hell (Matthew 25:41).

2. <u>Purgatory</u>. Some churches believe that when people die, they go to an intermediate place like purgatory to be cleansed from their sins. But the Bible says that after people die, they will immediately be judged (Hebrews 9:27), and they will go into either heaven or hell.

3. <u>No Eternal Hell</u>. Some churches believe that hell is not eternal. But the Bible says eternity is the same duration for the righteous in heaven and the wicked in hell (Daniel 12:2).

4. <u>Annihilation of the Wicked</u>. Some churches believe that the souls of the lost will cease to exist. But the

Bible says that hell is eternal, conscious torment (Jude 7).

Revelation 20:11-12
1. On what basis will believers be judged?
2. On what basis will unbelievers be judged?
3. Can anyone be saved by their works?

Matthew 25:31-33
1. Why are believers symbolized by sheep?
2. Why are unbelievers symbolized by goats?
3. Is Jesus Christ exclusive?
4. Is Jesus Christ tolerant?
5. Is the love of God revealed in judgment?

Hebrews 9:27
1. When will judgment happen?
2. What does this judgment determine?

John 5:28-29, Matthew 10:28
1. What is the resurrection of condemnation?
2. What kind of bodies will unbelievers receive at the resurrection?
3. In what way will bodies be destroyed in hell?

Matthew 18:8, Matthew 25:46, John 3:16, John 10:28
How do we know that hell is eternal?

2 Thessalonians 1:9

If something is eternally destroyed, what will that be like?

Daniel 12:2

1. What is everlasting contempt?
2. Is eternal hell fair? Why or why not?

Mark 9:44, Matthew 13:50, Revelation 14:11

1. What is hell like?
2. Why is there fire in hell?
3. If someone digs deep enough in the ground, will they find hell?

Luke 16:24

1. Are the souls in hell in conscious pain?
2. What is it like to have no rest?

Revelation 21:8

What is brimstone?

Luke 10:14

1. Are there levels in hell?
2. What will the best part of hell be like?
3. Who will be in the worst part of hell?
4. Why do people sometimes joke about a party in hell?

2 Corinthians 5:11, Jude 22-23

1. Can the reality of hell be used for evangelism?

2. Did Jesus ever warn unbelievers about hell? Should we?

Romans 14:12
What does it mean to give an account of yourself?

Matthew 12:36
Why are words so important for judgment?

2 Corinthians 5:9-10
Are you living in light of the fact that you will someday stand before God to be judged?

2 Corinthians 3:12-15
1. What kind of fire will test the work that we have done on the earth?
2. How can we be sure that what we are doing is of eternal value?
3. How can we avoid wasting our lives?

Crash Course in The Bible

THE BIBLE IS INERRANT, which means it doesn't make any mistakes. In whatever subject it touches, whether religion, history, or science, the Bible is perfect. It's perfect because it's written by God.

"All Scripture is God-breathed" (2 Timothy 3:16a).

God wrote the Bible through people.

"Holy men of God spoke as they were moved by the Holy Spirit" (2 Pet. 1:21).

Over a period of approximately 1,500 years, the Bible was written by 40 different inspired authors. The Bible is a big book made up of 66 smaller books.

The 66 books of the Bible were recognized by the early church as being the only books that were written by God. No other books in the world had the same quality as these books. When we read the Bible, the Holy Spirit will witness that these books are written by God. No other book carries the same spiritual quality as the Bible. Ancient pseudo-gospels like the Gospel of Thomas are of a completely different quality than the books of the Bible.

Reading the Bible

Each Christian needs to study the Bible for themselves and should read through the entire Bible at least once. When we read through the Bible, God's word will get into our minds and hearts. As we continue reading the Bible, the different parts of the Bible will begin to supernaturally connect through the help of the Holy Spirit.

"Man shall not live by bread alone, but by every word that proceeds from the mouth of God" (Matthew 4:4).

The word of God is spiritual food. We need spiritual food to feed our spirits, just as we need natural food to feed our bodies.

Reading the Bible should be a joy. We should *want* to read the Bible. Hungry people eat. They don't need to force food down their throats. We need to desire the word of God more than TV, internet, or other books and magazines. God can give us a supernatural hunger for the Bible. We should pray for this spiritual hunger. "God, give me a hunger and thirst for your word!" When we have a spiritual hunger for the Bible, it becomes easy to read.

Understanding the Bible

There will be passages in the Bible that we don't understand. Pray for understanding. The Holy Spirit will help you understand the word of God.

With our minds alone, we can't understand the Bible.

> But the natural man does not receive the things of the Spirit of God, for they are foolishness to him; nor can he know them, because they are spiritually discerned. (1 Corinthians 2:14)

We need the Holy Spirit to teach us the word of God.

"No prophecy of the Scripture is of any private interpretation" (2 Peter 1:20).

The Bible is not really "open to interpretation." It's not up to people to decide what the Bible means. It's up to God. God's interpretation of the Bible is the only one that matters. If we wonder what the Bible means, we need to study it more and pray. Hopefully, we will find good teachers who will accurately expound the Bible, but people can be wrong. Nothing can substitute for reading the Bible and understanding it through the help of the Holy Spirit.

The Bible interprets the Bible. One verse will illuminate another verse. Several passages about the same topic will give a fuller picture of what God is saying about that topic. To find these related verses, use cross-references. These references show how verses in different parts of the Bible connect. Ultimately, one author, God, wrote the entire Bible, and the whole book connects together supernaturally. For example, the book of Daniel illuminates Revelation, and vice versa.

Sometimes, to understand the meaning of a passage, it is necessary to refer to the original Biblical languages—Greek and Hebrew. There are nuances in these original languages that are impossible to fully capture in English, and only by looking at the original languages can these nuances be discovered. Learning Greek and Hebrew is ideal for a serious Bible student, but if this is not possible, there are many free software programs that make it easy to discover the meaning of specific Greek and Hebrew words.

The Difference Between the Old and New Testaments

Some parts of the Bible are literal, and some are symbolic. When studying the Bible, it is important not to take as literal what is symbolic, and not take as symbolic what is literal. If God has given us a literal command, we need to obey it. If he's given us a symbolic statement, we need to interpret it.

The teachings of Jesus and his apostles are literally applicable for us today, and we must follow them. Their instructions are the framework for the kingdom of God upon the earth. These words of the New Testament will judge us all (John 12:28).

The Old Testament, on the other hand, is mostly symbolic for us today. Full of wars, rituals, and religious pageantry, we learn from the Old Testament today not by following its specific examples or instructions, but by interpreting its symbols.

"All these things happened to them as examples, and they were written for our admonition" (1 Corinthians 10:11).

Most Mosaic laws are not to be followed literally by God's people today. When Christ came, he set us free from following the Mosaic law.

> For He Himself is our peace, who has made both one, and has broken down the middle wall of separation, having abolished in His flesh the enmity, that is, the law of commandments contained in ordinances, so as to create in Himself one new man from the two, thus making peace, and that He might reconcile them both to God in one body through the cross, thereby putting to death the enmity. (Ephesians 2:14-16)

Jesus set us free from the law because he fulfilled it by living a perfect life. Then he died, giving us the free gift of righteousness. Through the cross, he set us free from the law of Moses.

When Jesus began his ministry, he said,

> Do not think that I came to destroy the Law or the Prophets. I did not come to destroy but to fulfill. For assuredly, I say to you, till heaven and earth pass away, one jot or one tittle will by no means pass from the law till all is fulfilled. (Matthew 5:17-18)

Jesus said that he came to fulfill the law. He fulfilled it in two ways. First, he performed all the righteous requirements of the law. Second, he fulfilled the prophecies contained in the law.

One prophecy in the law about Christ says this:

> I will raise up for them a Prophet like you from among their brethren, and will put My words in His mouth, and He shall speak to them all that I command Him. And it shall be that whoever will not hear My words, which He speaks in My name, I will require it of him. (Deuteronomy 18:18-19)

In this passage, Moses spoke about Jesus Christ. He said that Jesus would speak the word of God.

Jesus spoke the powerful words of God. He revealed the commands of the kingdom of God. Jesus spoke many of these commands in Matthew 5-7, the Sermon on the Mount.

Jesus refers to his own commands when he says:

> Whoever therefore breaks one of the least of these commandments, and teaches men so, shall be called least in the kingdom of heaven; but whoever does and teaches them, he shall be called great in the kingdom of heaven. (Matthew 5:19)

"These commandments" refer to Jesus' own teachings, many of which he spoke in Matthew 5-7.

Our *position* in the kingdom of heaven ("great" or "least") is determined by our level of submission to Jesus while we live upon the earth. Our *entrance* into the kingdom of heaven is determined by whether or not we believe in the blood of Christ to take away our sins.

Jesus fulfilled the law. With the law fulfilled, we are no longer under its power. That is why it is said that the Law has been "abolished" through Christ (Ephesians 2:15). The Mosaic law has been annulled.

> For on the one hand there is an annulling of the former commandment because of its weakness and unprofitableness. (Hebrews 7:18)

Although the Law is annulled by the work of Christ, we must still obey some of the Law's commands, such as don't steal, kill, or commit adultery. This is not because we are still under the Mosaic Law, but because these commands have been reiterated to us in the New Testament. In the New Testament, these commands were not only reiterated by Jesus, but they were brought to a higher level. Adultery became something in the heart, not just the body; murder was no longer merely physical, but it became hatred.

Nine of the Ten Commandments were reiterated by Christ and his apostles. The remaining one, the literal observance of the Sabbath Day, was not reiterated. In the New Covenant, we are no longer under obligation to literally observe the Sabbath day.

We don't pick and choose what parts of the Law we want to follow. The entire Law has been abolished in Christ. Now we follow Jesus' New Testament commands by the power of his Spirit.

Old Testament Holidays

"So let no one judge you in food or in drink, or regarding a festival or a new moon or sabbaths, which are a shadow of things to come, but the substance is of Christ" (Colossians 2:16-17).

All Old Testament holidays, including the Sabbath Day, are shadows of Christ. They illuminate different aspects of Christ's work in our lives. For example, the Sabbath symbolizes resting in God and doing only the works that God wants us to do (see Hebrews 3 and 4). Jesus always kept the Sabbath, not by doing nothing one day a week like the Pharisees expected, but by doing what God wanted 24 hours a day, 7 days a week.

Observing Old Testament holidays literally today produces bondage.

> But now after you have known God, or rather are known by God, how is it that you turn again to the weak and beggarly elements, to which you desire again to be in bondage? You observe days and months and seasons and years. I am afraid for you, lest I have labored for you in vain. (Galatians 4:9-11)

Jesus came to fulfill the Old Testament and become the fullness of which the Law was a mere shadow. In fulfilling the Law, he took it out of the way for us, replacing it with the higher instructions of the kingdom of God. He brought the full revelation of the Spirit, which eliminated the shadows of the Old Testament.

To accurately apply the Old Testament to our lives today, we need to learn by the Holy Spirit how to interpret and apply its symbolic meaning.

Other Old Testament Shadows

The Mosaic law commanded God's people not to eat certain types of meat, including pork (Deuteronomy 14:8). But this has changed now.

God gave Peter a vision of animals descending in a sheet in Acts 10:11-15. The law said many of these animals were unclean, but God told Peter to eat them anyway.

Jesus said that all meats were clean, including pork, "because it does not enter his heart but his stomach, and is eliminated, thus purifying all foods" (Mark 7:19).

Paul told us to "eat whatever is sold in the meat market, asking no questions for conscience' sake" (1 Corinthians 10:25).

God doesn't even want us obeying basic Old Testament commands like circumcision. "If you become circumcised,

Christ will profit you nothing" (Galatians 5:2). Circumcision was one of the most important commands in the Old Testament, but it's not a command that we should keep today.

"Circumcision is nothing, and uncircumcision is nothing, but keeping the commandments of God is what matters" (1 Corinthians 7:19).

The commandments we must follow are all found in the New Testament. The Old Testament commands are types and shadows that reveal New Testament truths. The Old Testament helps us understand the gospel through its symbolic teaching.

"But we know that the law is good if one uses it lawfully" (1 Timothy 1:8).

The Old Testament symbols, whether incense, candles, vestments, religious buildings, musical instruments, or sacrifices, have all passed away. They provide a wealth of insight into Christ, who is our spiritual inheritance, and into God's plans for the advancement of his kingdom upon the earth. They are symbols for the church today. Both the Old Testament and the New Testament are invaluable for us, for they reveal the riches of Christ. But they reveal him in different ways.

PART II. Bible Preservation

It is important for each Christian to know that the Bible we have today is an accurate reflection of the original writings. God preserved his word carefully throughout history and has ensured that the Bible we have today is reliable.

The Old Testament was preserved over the centuries by Hebrew scribes called Masoretes. Their scribal diligence made sure that each copy they made of the Hebrew Bible was an exact copy of the originals. Because of their diligence, the copy of the Hebrew Bible we have today is the same as the one God originally gave to the original authors.

The New Testament was preserved with similar care. Dedicated scribes copied the apostolic writings and distributed them throughout the early churches. There are more ancient copies of the New Testament than any other piece of ancient literature. All these copies are in remarkable agreement, and none of the slight differences among them calls into question any of the fundamental doctrines of Christianity.

The earliest copies of the New Testament come from the first part of the second century. These extremely early copies reveal that the New Testament was written within the lifetimes of the first apostles, by the apostles themselves, and by their associates Mark, Luke, and Jude.

Textus Receptus

Throughout the centuries, the Greek New Testament was handed down among God's people— from church to church and from generation to generation. God supernaturally watched over his word, ensuring that accurate copies of the Bible were distributed among the churches. Scribes took their copying work seriously, recognizing that they were copying the inspired words of the Holy Spirit.

While errors occasionally cropped up in individual copies of the New Testament, these errors could be identified by comparing those copies with the many other copies that were accepted and used by the churches (in multiple languages and regions). Faulty copies were recognized and rejected. Reliable copies were used and spread. A system of checks and balances, along with the guidance of the Holy Spirit, kept the Scriptures pure from defect.

The ancient manuscript tradition used by churches throughout history has come down to us today in the form of the Greek manuscript called the Textus Receptus. *Textus Receptus* is Latin for *Received Text*. This manuscript tradition can also be called the Majority Text, for the vast majority of ancient New Testament Greek manuscripts generally reflect its readings. The Textus Receptus is the Greek manuscript that was used by reformers like Martin Luther and William Tyndale. It forms the basis for the King James Bible. It is the Greek manuscript that was in use throughout history, preserved by God among his people until today.

Rise of Liberal Scholarship and the Critical Text

In the 1800s, skepticism about the Bible began to rise in European and North American universities. Liberal scholars began questioning many things about basic Christianity. They doubted whether Jesus was God, whether he was born of a virgin, whether he worked miracles, and whether he resurrected. They also began doubting whether God really preserved the Bible, whether the Bible was infallible, and whether the Textus Receptus was reliable.

Out of this skeptical atmosphere emerged a new field of study called Textual Criticism. Textual critics came to believe that God did not preserve his word among his people. They didn't trust the versions that were copied and handed down by the churches throughout history. Instead, they thought that *they* had to determine which Greek manuscripts most accurately reflected God's original word. Textual critics began standing over the word of God

— criticizing it— in order to determine what should be in the Bible and what shouldn't. They began to pick and choose which words and verses should be in the Bible and which ones shouldn't.

Critical scholars soon developed their own Greek New Testament to replace the Textus Receptus. This new Greek Text was based primarily on two newly discovered manuscripts— one from the Vatican and one from a monastery in the Sinai Peninsula. Largely on the basis of these two manuscripts (both of which are riddled with errors), they reconstructed the Greek New Testament. This new text was called the Critical Text.

Textus Receptus vs. Critical Text

Today, the Textus Receptus and the Critical Text are the two primary Greek manuscripts that underlie various modern English New Testaments. Some versions are based on the Textus Receptus, and some are based on the Critical Text. The differences between these two Greek texts are not large, and they do not affect any major issues of the faith.

However, there are significant differences between the Critical Text and the Textus Receptus. For example, the Critical Text omits at least 16 verses completely from the New Testament, including Matthew 17:21: "However, this kind does not go out except by prayer and fasting." Try looking up Matt. 17:21, 18:11, 23:14, Mark 7:16, 9:44, 9:46, 11:26, 15:28, Luke 17:36, 23:17, John 5:4, Acts 8:37, 15:34, 24:7, 28:29, and Rom. 16:24 in the ESV, a popular modern version based on the Critical Text, and you'll find these verses are missing. Many other important verses are drastically changed, like Rom. 8:1 and 1 John 5:7. There are many other places in the Critical Text where important words are missing, such as *Lord* or *Christ* when referring to Jesus.

We don't want to miss anything from God's word.

The Bible is God's word, and it is inerrant. His supernatural care is involved in its preservation. If we believe that God perfectly preserved his infallible word among his people since the apostolic days, we must believe that the Textus Receptus accurately reflects the word of God.

To prefer the Critical Text is to believe that liberal scholars of the 1800s somehow restored the inerrant word of God to the church. This strains credulity. This is not how God worked with the Old Testament, and it's not how he worked with the New Testament.

The Textus Receptus reflects the manuscripts used by God's people from the apostolic times. It was used by the majority of God's people throughout history and has the bulk of manuscript support today. An English version based on the Textus Receptus will give us confidence that our English Bible is the inerrant word of God.

The major Bible translations today in English that are based on the Textus Receptus are the KJV, NKJV, and MEV. These are the most accurate of the widely known modern English versions.

Visit

www.bethelcornerstone.org

More books by Peter John Brooks:

Three Marys

Spiritual Technology

Where God is King

The Coming Glory

Goat Tags

Absurd Christianity

www.ingramcontent.com/pod-product-compliance
Lightning Source LLC
Chambersburg PA
CBHW061155120626
46546CB00005B/2070